*THE FUTURE*

# WOMEN
## *Who LEAD*

**Jennifer Lara, Hanna Olivas and Angela Bell**
Along With 27 Other Inspiring Women

© 2023 ALL RIGHTS RESERVED.
Published by She Rises Studios Publishing www.SheRisesStudios.com.

No part of this book may be reproduced or transmitted in any form whatsoever, electronic, or mechanical, including photocopying, recording, or by any informational storage or retrieval system without the expressed written, dated and signed permission from the publisher and co-authors.

LIMITS OF LIABILITY/DISCLAIMER OF WARRANTY:

The co-authors and publisher of this book have used their best efforts in preparing this material. While every attempt has been made to verify the information provided in this book, neither the co-authors nor the publisher assumes any responsibility for any errors, omissions, or inaccuracies.

The co-authors and publisher make no representation or warranties with respect to the accuracy, applicability, or completeness of the contents of this book. They disclaim any warranties (expressed or implied), merchantability, or for any purpose. The co-authors and publisher shall in no event be held liable for any loss or other damages, including but not limited to special, incidental, consequential, or other damages.

ISBN: 978-1-960136-40-4

## Table of Contents

INTRODUCTION ................................................................. 7

REWRITING MY STORY: TRANSFORMING FROM SCAPEGOAT TO THRIVING CEO
   By Jennifer Lara ........................................................ 10

INSPIRE AND EMPOWER YOURSELF
   By Hanna Olivas ........................................................ 19

CREATING AND LEADING FROM A QUIET PLACE
   By Angela Bell .......................................................... 22

YOUR JOURNEY, YOUR SYMPHONY
   By Adriana Luna Carlos ............................................. 31

UNCOVERING THE TRUTH - A HEALING JOURNEY BEYOND BIG PHARMA
   By Alexa Elbrader ..................................................... 39

I CHOOSE TO BELIEVE
   By Sarah Whyte ........................................................ 49

PASSION, A PEN, AND THE COLLECTED WISDOM OF MY PAST
   By Christi Pratte ....................................................... 55

BIRTH IN POWER- AWAKEN YOUR INTUITION AND RECLAIM YOUR MOTHERLY INSTINCTS
   By Ilka Bee .............................................................. 64

SHADOWS AND LIGHT
   By Andrea Mostaffa .................................................. 71

THE POWER OF A MOTHER'S LOVE: MY DRIVING FORCE
By Elizabeth Valle .................................................................. 78

NOT ASHAMED
By Jamie Mychelle Faulcon ..................................................... 84

THE GREY UNICORN
By Diana Svensson ................................................................. 91

WIIFT (WHAT'S IN IT FOR THEM) IT'S WHAT I LIVE BY
By Grainne Fletcher ................................................................ 98

ANOTHER BUSINESS AGAIN?
By Londell J Cox .................................................................. 104

THE POWER SOURCE: HOW I FOUND FREEDOM FROM IMPOSTER SYNDROME BY LEARNING TO TRUST MYSELF
By Prudence Hatchett ............................................................ 110

I FINALLY GOT OUT OF MY OWN WAY
By Nicole Villanueva .............................................................. 116

THERE'S JUST NOT ENOUGH TIME
By Gina Stockdall .................................................................. 121

MORE FEMALE HEADLINERS: APPLY WITHIN
By Samantha Bearman ........................................................... 126

A VIKING FUNERAL
By Lorena Coreas .................................................................. 132

SHE'S SO, COMO SE DICE… LUCKY!
By Jasmin Valdez ................................................................... 137

FROM DREAMER TO ENTREPRENEUR
By Gabby Gutierrez ............................................................... 143

WE ALL DREAM IN DIFFERENT LANGUAGES
By Julissa Sanchez ................................................................. 149

THANKS TO HER
By Samantha Holm................................................................. 157

THE POWER OF BREAKING FREE: LETTING GO OF HIGH
CONTROL RELIGION
By Laura Miramontes............................................................... 163

STORY BEHIND THE BRAND: PEACE HEALTH ENJOY
By Irene Karpadaki.................................................................. 171

BREAKING GENERATIONAL CHAINS
By Lourdes Auquilla................................................................ 178

THE MAGIC OF NOSOTRAS
By Irisneri Alicea ..................................................................... 184

BREAKING FREE
By Jacklyn Collins.................................................................... 190

ADMIRING THE THORN OF A ROSE
By Cynthia Puga ..................................................................... 197

MY CHINGONA ERA: A JOURNEY OF RESILIENCE AND
SELF-DISCOVERY
By Sandra Nuñez .................................................................... 202

# INTRODUCTION

## Women Who Lead - The Future of Entrepreneurship

Step into the transformational world of female entrepreneurship as you delve into the pages of "Women Who Lead - The Future of Entrepreneurship." This remarkable book isn't just a source of knowledge; it's a captivating journey that unveils a treasure trove of insights and motivation, meticulously curated by 30 distinguished experts. Their collective wisdom is poised to empower you with the finest strategies, invaluable wisdom, and unwavering motivation, serving as the fuel for your relentless pursuit of personal and professional growth.

Within these pages, you will embark on a transformative voyage, one that promises not only self-discovery but also profound empowerment. Here, the narratives of extraordinary women take center stage, women whose indomitable spirit propelled them to overcome great life obstacles, paving the way for the creation of influential, world-altering enterprises. These women, through their journeys, become beacons of hope and inspiration, guiding you through the often intricate and challenging landscape of entrepreneurship.

"Women Who Lead" is more than a mere compilation of stories; it's a testament to the resilience of the human spirit. It illuminates the undeniable truth that our most extraordinary triumphs frequently emerge from the crucible of life's most formidable trials. These stories serve as mirrors, reflecting your own potential and resilience, inspiring you to push boundaries and achieve greatness in your own entrepreneurial endeavors.

So, turn these pages with anticipation and curiosity. Allow the stories and insights contained within to shape your perspective and fuel your ambitions. This isn't just a book; it's a transformative experience, an opportunity to learn from the best, to discover your inner strength, and to embrace the future of entrepreneurship with unwavering determination.

"Women Who Lead" is your invitation to join a community of trailblazing women who have dared to dream, overcome, and succeed. It's a declaration that your journey, like theirs, can be marked by resilience, empowerment, and profound achievement. So, let the journey begin – your future in entrepreneurship awaits, and it's brighter than ever before.

## Jennifer Lara

CEO of Femme Sales Mastery Academy

https://www.linkedin.com/in/jenniferlara509/
https://www.facebook.com/iamjenlara
https://www.instagram.com/iamjenlara/
www.iamjenlara.com

Meet Jennifer Lara, a marketing and sales strategist, speaker, accomplished author, and a dedicated mother.

Jennifer is driven by a powerful mission: she aims to empower women on a global scale, guiding them towards creating the impactful online businesses of their dreams. Central to her expertise is the art of developing and implementing highly effective marketing strategies to reach a broader audience and create a greater impact.

She focuses on building authentic relationships and equips women with the tools and insights necessary to navigate the business world successfully.

Through her mentorship, women are not only equipped with practical skills but are also inspired to embrace their potential fully. She transforms dreams into tangible achievements, leaving a trail of successful and empowered women entrepreneurs in her wake.

# REWRITING MY STORY: TRANSFORMING FROM SCAPEGOAT TO THRIVING CEO

By Jennifer Lara

Let me paint you a picture of my upbringing – a masterpiece that starred yours truly as the ultimate rebel, the chief troublemaker, the one with all the sass. And in the grand spectacle of my family dynamics, I was the star of the show – the 'scapegoat,' the 'black sheep.' Those are the labels they slapped on me, labels that once made me question my very essence. My upbringing was like being trapped in a maze of restrictions, a life where everyone else held the pen to my story except for me. This started a journey of transformation that would flip the script of my life. So, lean in, because I'm about to spill the tea on how I seized control, rewrote my own narrative, and emerged as the author of my own destiny. Join me as we explore a world where anything is possible for ambitious women like us!

First off, when I graduated from college, I had no idea that my life would take the journey it has—from financial services professional to entrepreneur, author, and speaker. I'm proud of all the lessons learned, successes earned, and inspiring stories shared on this incredible path of business and freedom.

You see, my family clung to some rather restrictive beliefs, deeply rooted in their upbringing on a small ranch in Mexico. Their lives were shaped by the heavy burden of poverty, scarce resources, and a lack of educational opportunities. Though, my story took a different turn because I was the first generation in my family to be raised in the United States. It was here I got to see a different perspective.

The contrast between how my brothers and I were raised couldn't have been more glaring. I was practically under house arrest – no going out, no dating; I was the designated household babysitter and cleaning czar.

One vivid memory stands out: I was elbow-deep in laundry on a Friday night, when I saw my brother getting ready to go out. Unable to contain my frustration, I blurted out, "Hey, why do you get to go out while I'm stuck here doing laundry?" His response, seared into my memory, "Because you're a GIRL." And with that, he went out the door. My stomach churned like a whirlpool. I frequently protested these restrictions and the unfairness. This caused constant clashes between my family and I. They would often use words to describe me such as:

"You're so difficult."

"Why can't you be more like so-and-so?"

"Girls aren't supposed to do that."

To them, my behavior seemed entirely unruly, and I didn't conform to their expectations of being a "well-behaved" girl as they had hoped for. To this day, my mother still believes I'm an "angry person." But what she clearly missed is that I'm not the type to sit idly by while injustice frolics around. I was always rolling up my sleeves and diving headfirst into protest mode.

Yet, my culture isn't the only one throwing this party. Around the globe, women have often been handed the same script: be sweet, be accommodating, and fit into that neat little box of expectations. They'd find themselves stuck, like a glitch in a never-ending loop, with about as much influence over their lives as a potted plant. My story? It's just a mix of the tales of countless women worldwide who have had a similar experience.

However, this ended for me at 18 when I finally escaped to college at the University of Washington in Seattle. I started going to therapy and reading more and more books. I had this epiphany that the never-ending battles with my family weren't some reflection of my worth, but a mirror reflecting the constraints placed on them by the same

Women Who Lead | 11

patriarchal society that had stifled generations of women before me. Just echoes of a cycle I was absolutely determined to shatter. It was then that I decided I was going to start crafting a life for myself bursting with opportunities, adorned with accomplishments, and soaked in a profound sense of purpose.

So fresh out of college, I did exactly that. I plunged into the financial world, unlocking a great understanding of money's role in the world. Money is a tool and a medium of exchange. This knowledge allowed me to create more value in others' lives and live a fulfilling one myself. Money, you see, is a crucial player in our lives, thriving when we create a balance between spending, saving, investing, and giving back. This holistic approach, spanning physical, emotional, and spiritual, helps us become better versions of ourselves, creating a positive ripple effect in our communities, relationships, and families. It was this revelation that ignited the entrepreneur in me! I knew I needed to surround myself with women who were equally passionate visionaries. When I started doing that I realized there were so many women out there ambitious, passionate, and visionary souls, all sharing this same burning passion for crafting a better world.

Still, many of these remarkable women needed the tools, the guidance, and the support to turn their visions into tangible, world-altering businesses. That's when it struck me: I could be the bridge, the catalyst for their transformative journey. Learning to master the art of leadership and using the power of social media marketing were the keys to creating the impactful businesses of their dreams. Sharing my knowledge and expertise, I aimed to empower women to transform their unique skills into careers and businesses that not only provide income but also lead to lives filled with abundance, choice, and freedom.

With every client I've worked with, with every workshop I've led, and with every coaching session, I've seen incredible transformations. I've seen world-changers rise to the occasion, creating ripple effects of change that touch lives across the globe. As we witness a growing number of women wholeheartedly pursuing education, fearlessly taking on their dream careers, and boldly launching their own businesses, a great transformation is unfolding in our world. Women are leaving an indelible mark on the workforce, spanning and bridging diverse gaps, and contributing in countless meaningful ways.

Including but not limited to:

- **Innovation:** Women are at the forefront of driving innovation and entrepreneurship across a multitude of industries. Their startups are infusing the market with fresh perspectives, groundbreaking ideas, and revolutionary products or services. This not only sparks economic growth but also lights up the job market with exciting opportunities.

- **Diversity and Inclusion:** Women mean business when it comes to diversity and inclusion. They are great at assembling diverse teams and creating work environments that are bursting with creativity. This magnetizes a broader talent pool and raises the overall company performance meter.

- **Mentorship and Support:** Women are passionate about supporting and mentoring others, fostering the development of future female leaders and entrepreneurs. They provide guidance, networks, and resources to help other women succeed in their careers or start their businesses.

- **Closing the Gender Pay Gap**: By establishing their businesses, female entrepreneurs often have more control over their earnings and are better positioned to close the gender pay gap within their organizations. They can set fair compensation practices and lead by example in paying employees equitably.

- **Flexible Work Environments:** Female business owners are more likely to implement flexible work policies, such as remote work options and flexible hours. This flexibility helps employees achieve a better work-life balance, which can be especially beneficial for working mothers and fathers.

- **Community Engagement:** Many female business owners are deeply involved in their communities. They support local initiatives, charities, and social causes, which can have a positive impact on the well-being of their employees and the community at large.

- **Addressing Social and Environmental Issues:** Female-led businesses often prioritize social and environmental responsibility. They integrate sustainability practices into their operations, contributing to a more sustainable future and addressing critical global issues.

- **Advocating for Equal Opportunities:** Female-led businesses are big on social and environmental responsibility. They make sustainability a part of their mission, contributing to a greener, more sustainable future, and taking on global issues head-on.

Despite being labeled as "too loud," "too bossy," or "too difficult," many of these remarkable women fought their way to the top. Now, female business owners are not just crushing it in building profitable empires; they are also leading vital social transformations. Their resilience is not just reshaping the workforce; it's bridging critical gaps in business and the world. Their strength paves the way for a more inclusive and empowered future!

*Now ladies, armed with this knowledge, allow me to impart some invaluable advice on how you too can construct & GROW a purposeful and lucrative business that not only brings you immense joy but also grants you the authority to shape your own story:*

- **Discover Your Passion and Purpose:** Take time to introspect and uncover what genuinely inspires and motivates you, embracing the causes, values, or issues that deeply resonate with your core, while recognizing your distinct skills, talents, and strengths.

- **Become An Expert In A Field That Ignites Your Passion:** This will not only benefit your career but will also help you niche down and position yourself as a sought-after authority, opening doors to new clients, higher income, and lasting impact in your chosen area of expertise!

- **Create a Valuable And "No Brainer" Offer:** Your product is your service and it is what you will EXCHANGE with another to create income in your business. Your OFFER is how you present it. Your offer is the bridge between your product and your customers, the vehicle that transports your creation into their lives, and the catalyst that turns a casual observer into a satisfied customer. It's the difference between merely having something to sell and crafting an irresistible proposition that compels people to say, "Yes, I want that!"

- **Branding:** Absolutely, your online presence is your lifeline in the digital world. Your brand isn't just a logo or a product – it's the essence of your identity, the magnet that draws in ATTENTION. In the vast sea of online entrepreneurs, getting noticed is the first battle won. Without that initial intrigue and a compelling reason for your audience to dive deeper, making sales becomes an uphill struggle.

- **Establish a Sales Process:** One of the common pitfalls for many business owners is the neglect of building a structured sales pipeline. But here's the deal: this pipeline isn't just a map; it's the master plan for smoothly guiding individuals from their initial interaction with your brand through to the successful delivery of your products or services. It encompasses various crucial components such as your marketing and promotional strategies (including social media and advertising efforts), enticing free offers, the seamless integration of automation, the design and optimization of effective sales funnels, and, finally, the seamless execution of product or service delivery. Establishing a well-defined sales process incorporating these elements is integral to the success and sustainability of your business!

- **Mastery of Marketing:** Regardless of how exceptional your product may be, it can remain hidden without effective marketing and promotion. Marketing and promotion are what illuminate your product, drawing people toward your business and product while igniting their curiosity and desire to work with you!

- **Exceptional Delivery:** Every year we have new clients that come from referrals! When it comes to your offer delivery, consider it the VIP treatment for your clients! We're all about serving up responses and information so finely tuned to your needs that they practically do a victory dance when they hit your inbox. It's all served up on a silver platter, concise and crystal clear, right on schedule, and with a dash of reliability. The aim? To leave them in awe, scratching their head, wondering how they ever got by without your service – now that's what we call exceeding expectations!

So, ladies, take note and watch the magic happen! With these tips, you'll be empowering yourselves and your fellow women, creating an environment that's all about success and inclusivity – whether you're conquering personal or professional challenges! It's amazing to watch the transformative power of women as they take control of their destinies, crafting lives of health, wealth, and fulfillment. I am driven to ensure that women worldwide no longer dream in silence but dare to dream out loud. Together, we are rewriting the narrative, transforming dreams into reality, and building a world where women stand tall, unyielding, and unstoppable to create the greatest ripples in the world. I believe every woman deserves the chance to break free from the narratives that once confined them. In doing so, they can pave the way for future generations, creating a legacy of empowerment, independence, and self-discovery!

Fast forward to today — my story? Oh, it's a whole new path! Throughout my journey of empowerment and self-love, I've been on a mission to pave a path where my little ones know their worth stretches as wide as the universe. And their dreams and desires are like shooting stars on a clear night – entirely within their grasp. This transformation isn't just for me; it's healing for the souls of my ancestors, and it's tearing down the walls of a world where daughters aren't seen as burdens but as fierce sources of unstoppable strength and change!

Finally, I share my story in hopes that it helps others unleash their potential and claim their rightful place in a world where they are the authors of their own destinies. Today I look back on my journey and I am filled with gratitude and a deep sense of purpose. Building impactful businesses has helped me transform the world as my canvas. I now get to enjoy the freedom to travel with my loving family, including my partner, my almost three-year-old son, and the little life growing within me as I write this and embrace the magic of pregnancy at 37 weeks and I can do this once again – because I am a GIRL!

## Hanna Olivas

Founder & CEO of She Rises Studios
Podcast & TV Host | Best Selling Author | Influential Speaker | Blood Cancer Advocate | #BAUW Movement Creator

https://www.linkedin.com/company/she-rises-studios/
https://www.instagram.com/sherisesstudios
https://www.facebook.com/sherisesstudios
www.SheRisesStudios.com

Author, Speaker, and Founder. Hanna was born and raised in Las Vegas, Nevada, and has paved her way to becoming one of the most influential women of 2022. Hanna is the co-founder of She Rises Studios and the founder of the Brave & Beautiful Blood Cancer Foundation. Her journey started in 2017 when she was first diagnosed with Multiple Myeloma, an incurable blood cancer. Now more than ever, her focus is to empower other women to become leaders because The Future is Female. She is currently traveling and speaking publicly to women to educate them on entrepreneurship, leadership, and owning the female power within.

# INSPIRE AND EMPOWER YOURSELF

By Hanna Olivas

Dream Big, Do Bigger. It sounds so cliché, right?

Not when you truly realize that you only have one life, not nine. You begin to make your dreams and goals a priority, not an option. Every thought and action causes a reaction, even when you are dreaming. So the real question is how to inspire and empower yourself to dream big and do bigger things in your life.

Allow me to take you on a journey to help answer these questions and get to the root of why so many of us never see our dreams come to fruition.

We are all born and die. Those are two things every single person can count on. It's the how and when that are different for each of us. We all have a limited time here on earth. So why waste even a single second living in fear, doubt, procrastination, or unhappiness? What can you do right now to change your perspective and outlook on life? First, you must make yourself a priority, from your health to your wealth. Do not ever take your health for granted, because in addition to only having one life, you only get one body, so handle it with care, prayer, and love. We must begin and end each day with positive and truthful intentions. You live your life on purpose. Those dreams in your heart are there for a reason, and it's your responsibility to find out how to make them happen and take even bigger actions to see them through.

Stay consistent in your personal journey. We can't expect to get the best results if we start, stop, start, and stop. The old saying "go big or go home" is so true. Many of us tend to forget that. When life takes us through different adventures, trials, and tribulations, that is when we truly begin to understand how valuable our time is. I believe most of us win or learn. There is no luck. Almost everything that happens is a direct reaction to our thoughts. So if our thoughts are negative, so are our actions. If our thoughts are positive, so are our actions. It's that simple. Our subconscious leads the way. So if we are dreaming about an amazing life and opportunities, we are inspiring and empowering ourselves subconsciously to make them a reality. It's your choice to choose one or the other, so choose wisely. How do you ask? What you watch, what you eat, your good or bad habits, who you associate with, what you listen to, etc. They all turn into thoughts, and thoughts turn into beliefs and actions. We can all have limitless possibilities. Most fail because none of us like the growing pains or the unknown. We like security and safety. It's just human nature and our brains' way of protecting us. So if you truly want to grow, you must be willing to get uncomfortable and reprogram your mindset to believe that anything is possible.

As you read all the different chapters in this book, I hope you find what you are looking for and create the life you want to live, not run from.

Have that honest conversation with yourself and decide what you really want in this life.

Stay inspired and empowered.

With Love,
Hanna

## Angela Bell

Founder & CEO The Inspired & Profitable Momprenuer

https://www.facebook.com/angela.bell.3597/
https://www.instagram.com/i.am.angelabell/
https://www.inspirednprofitablemompreneur.com/

Angela Bell is the founder of The Mom Magic Anthology Series and the Mom Magic Movement! She is also the founder and CEO at The Inspired & Profitable Mompreneur Business, Podcast, Magazine & TV Show.

Angela is on a mission to empower moms around the world to stand in their power, embrace their dreams, and create their own business!

Angela is a 6X International Best Seller, multi-passionate entrepreneur, business coach for moms, and mom of twins.

# CREATING AND LEADING FROM A QUIET PLACE

By Angela Bell

I enjoy silence. In fact, I often search for it.

I find it funny how uncomfortable silence can make people. I'm the opposite; idle chit-chat makes me uncomfortable. Loud noises and crowds make me uncomfortable. Too much noise makes it hard for me to hear my inner voice that speaks with universal wisdom.

My name is Angela, and I am what you'd call an empath and introvert. Most people who know me well don't think I'm an introvert, but that's just because I'm comfortable with them. I chose my circle carefully.

It took me a long time to accept my introversion and see it as a strength. I spent a lot of my life trying to learn to be loud, assert myself, call attention to myself, and control the conversation. But it always felt wrong and left me feeling drained.

Don't get me wrong - I love the spotlight when I feel called to take it. And I love to speak, share, and lead. I just like to do it in my own way and in my own time.

My way of being runs contrary to the noise and business of today. Everyone is yelling to be heard, forcing things to go their way, and asserting dominance and judgment over others. To be honest, I don't understand why they are exerting all that effort when there is a much easier way.

As I have begun to embrace my way of being and doing, I have found it has its own unique strengths and advantages. It feels better to me, creates an environment of peace, and accomplishes my daily goal to add more love and joy to the world.

Six key aspects of my personal style of leadership are:

- *Invite don't force.*
- *Listen to hear and learn, not to respond.*
- *If a solution is not win/win, everyone loses.*
- *I am not better or worse than anyone, just different.*
- *Remember, everyone has something to offer and something to teach you.*
- *My way is not the only way, nor is anyone else's.*

## Invite, Don't Force

Albert Einstein is quoted as saying, "Peace cannot be kept by force; it can only be achieved by understanding." I believe this quote can be applied universally. It has been shown that what we resist persists. When we try to force people or things to bend to our will, we are met with resistance. Whether this is regarding a world view, a task to be completed at the office, or with our children, when we try to force things to happen we are met with equal and opposite resistance.

I have lived my years of trying to force things. I tried to force success, force relationships to work, and force people to accept me, and all I got for it was frustration and crap self-esteem.

When we invite, open the door, and say "Hey, come check this out," we are saying nothing about the rightness or wrongness of what currently exists, and therefore, we are met with no resistance. Instead, we provoke curiosity and open up the lines for creative thinking. We create space for people to have their thoughts and opinions to invite them to change their minds. In short, it feels better, so it's easier.

## Listen to Hear and Learn, Not Respond

You can learn so much if you just listen. When I enter a new environment, I am often the quietest person in the room. It's not that

I don't have anything to say. It's just that I prefer to listen and observe. You can learn a lot about people and situations when you just listen. People's actions and ways of interacting will tell you more about them than their words. And if you listen intently enough, you can see the humanity in even the most abrasive person.

In today's society, everyone is so busy trying to be seen and heard that no one is seeing or hearing. We are desperately seeking someone, anyone, to acknowledge us and see us for who we really are. Most people are so busy preparing their responses that they never get around to hearing what the person in front of them is actually trying to say. Which is often "I'm here, I want to be seen. I want to be known and understood." I have found that the easiest way to become the most popular person in the room is to actively listen to people. While that is never my purpose, it's just a positive outcome.

I actually enjoy listening to people. I value their thoughts, experiences, and opinions, even if they differ from my own.

## If a Solution is Not Win/Win, Everyone Loses

My dad always told me to look for a win/win solution. This idea has always felt right to me. I have never been comfortable achieving or obtaining things if it was at someone else's expense.

I guess that's why the whole concept of competition rubs me the wrong way. It implies that for one person to win, another must lose. For one person to have, another must have not.

If we win at the expense of another, we have essentially made ourselves more important than them. Our wants and needs must be met at all costs. If anything, it shows the world our fears and insecurities, not our power and importance.

Finding a win/win solution isn't always the easiest way, nor is it the fastest way. It takes time, effort, and care. We have to be willing to listen to what the other party needs and why it matters to them. We have to value their needs as much as our own.

When we invest in finding win/win solutions, we invest in ourselves, our community, our teams, and our business. We do the work to benefit more than just ourselves. We add to the world instead of taking from it. And everyone benefits.

**I am Not Better or Worse than Anyone, Just Different**

Comparison is a constant in today's society. Everyone is looking at everyone else and measuring.

I compared myself to other people for years, never quite measuring up. Like I said, I have always been quiet. I have always liked what I liked, not what was popular. This led to a lot of instances where I felt like I wasn't good enough which led to shame.

It wasn't until I came to appreciate my uniqueness that I could let go of the shame. Once I stopped trying to be like everyone else and stopped trying to be accepted, I was able to accept myself. The funny part is, the more I accepted other people as they were without trying to change them or wishing they were different, the easier it became to accept myself. It's cyclical. When we love and accept ourselves, flaws and all, we can better love and accept others. When we realize that our differences make the world exciting, we stop trying to fit in and force others into a mold.

I will never ask someone to do something, in business or otherwise, that I am not willing to do myself. I do not think I am better or worse than anyone else. I am just uniquely me.

This experience made me very aware of how other people feel. I know what it's like to feel less than, so I work very hard to ensure I don't make people feel that way. This leads to a very important point...

### Everyone Has Something to Offer or Teach You

And yes, I mean EVERYONE. Even the person that drives you the craziest.

When we look for the good in people or the lesson from a situation, we reframe how we see the world. Instead of seeing "bad", we see interesting. Instead of seeing problems, we see questions. When we are willing to look for the good in people and what they have to offer, we make space for them to showcase their unique skills.

It's so easy to judge and write people off. It takes effort to give people time to shine. One of the gifts of being introverted is that I don't talk to fill space. This creates an opportunity for other people to talk, even if it's just to fill space. When I listen as they speak, I often get insights into what makes them special. And when I take the time to share my insights with them, I help them see it too.

Believe it or not, everyone wants to contribute; everyone wants to feel valuable. When we look for their value, we help them shine just a little bit brighter.

And the world gets a little bit better.

### My Way is Not the Only Way, Nor is Anyone Else's

This one was a hard one for me. I think A LOT, and because I think so much, I often think I know A LOT. This used to lead to me thinking I knew better than everyone else. I would get frustrated when people wouldn't listen or couldn't follow what I was thinking. The other challenge it would present is that I would follow MY way even when it wasn't working. I would try to force it. I had to prove to everyone else that I was right, I was worthy, and I had value.

It was exhausting.

Accepting my unique gifts and talents and accepting myself meant I stopped having to prove myself all the time and opened my eyes to the fact that there is no one right way. There are as many different ways to do things as there are people, and each one has value and can be successful. Someone else's way of doing things doesn't make mine bad, just different.

When I no longer needed to justify my existence, I opened up to trying new ways, some better, some not. But with each new experience, I learned more.

Accepting that my way wasn't the only way allowed me to ask for help and receive it. It has created more ease and flow in my life. I didn't need to be in charge all the time. It gave me more time to rest and recover, which is something a lot of us introverts need.

**Conclusion**

The world needs all kinds of people, and there is no one right way of being. As a leader and an introvert, it can sometimes feel like it would be easier if we were just a little louder, made a few more demands, or commanded more attention. But that simply isn't true.

One of the beautiful aspects of introverted leaders is that we can comfortably be our best selves while creating space for others to do the same. We can bring calm to chaotic situations. We give people time and space to breathe.

I also think we are a bit of a secret weapon. People often underestimate introverts for all the above-mentioned reasons. We don't call a lot of attention to ourselves, we contemplate and think to ourselves, and we don't share all of our inner thoughts. This, at times, takes the pressure off and gives us the space we need to create from our inner place of brilliance. When people already don't expect much, we don't have the added pressure of living up to expectations. This gives us the freedom to be creative and come up with unique solutions.

If you are reading this and are an introvert, I hope it has helped you see just how special and powerful you are. I hope it has encouraged you to shine in your unique way. And I hope it has helped you see that you are perfect just as you are!

Xo Angela

## Adriana Luna Carlos

Founder and CEO of She Rises Studios & FENIX TV

https://www.linkedin.com/in/adriana-luna-carlos/
https://www.facebook.com/adrianalunacarlos
https://www.instagram.com/sherisesstudios/
https://www.sherisesstudios.com/
https://www.srslatina.com/
https://fenixtv.app/

Adriana Luna Carlos is an accomplished web and graphic designer, author, and mentor with a passion for helping women succeed in life and business. With over 10 years of experience in graphic and web arts, Adriana has built a reputation as an innovative leader and entrepreneur. In 2020, she co-founded She Rises Studios, a multi-digital media company and publishing house that has helped countless clients achieve their branding and marketing goals. In 2023, she co-created FENIX TV, an online streaming platform that showcases stories of people breaking barriers, shattering stereotypes, and triumphing against the odds.

As an advocate for women's success, Adriana challenges her clients and mentees to strive for nothing less than excellence. She has a deep understanding of the insecurities and challenges that women often face in the business world and provides the guidance and resources needed to overcome them. Her success as a business leader and entrepreneur has made her a sought-after mentor and speaker at events around the world.

Through her work, Adriana has demonstrated a commitment to creating opportunities for women to succeed in business and life. Her passion for innovation, leadership, and women's empowerment has made her a respected figure in the business community, and her impact will undoubtedly continue to inspire and empower women for years to come.

# YOUR JOURNEY, YOUR SYMPHONY

By Adriana Luna Carlos

When we think about leadership, it's like remembering snapshots in a photo album – moments that stick with us and teach us important things. Looking back on my own journey, there are two stories that really stand out. These stories helped me understand what being a leader means and how I want to lead.

The first story takes me back to when I worked at a busy grocery store. There was this amazing manager who was totally different from the usual bosses. He didn't just tell us what to do; he worked alongside us. His attitude was incredible – always friendly and funny, making work enjoyable even when it was tough. He showed me that leadership is more than just giving orders; it's about working together and making everyone feel like they're part of a team.

Then there's another memory that's not so great. I used to work at a sign company, and my boss there was a bit of a micromanager. She would use cameras to watch everything we did, like she didn't trust us. I could hear the camera moving whenever I walked around the office. It was uncomfortable, and it made me realize that trust is a big part of good leadership.

Now, I don't just remember these stories for the memories. I use them to shape the way I lead. I treat my team with respect and try to understand their perspectives, just like that great manager did. And I avoid the micromanaging approach, focusing on trust instead.

As you think about your own journey, take a moment to remember instances where leadership played a role. Maybe it was during a school project where you guided a team to success or when you stepped up at a family event to keep things running smoothly. Think about how these moments shaped your understanding of leadership. Did they inspire you to collaborate more effectively, or did they ignite a desire to support others? Consider how these experiences continue to influence the way you manage people and situations today.

Our personal stories remind us that leadership isn't a one-size-fits-all concept. It's a blend of experiences, insights, and aspirations unique to each of us. As we explore the process of crafting our individual leadership styles, keep in mind that your journey, like mine, is woven with threads of growth, introspection, and a resolute commitment to inspire and make a positive impact.

## Understanding Different Leadership Styles

Throughout my journey, I've come across a variety of leadership styles, each leaving its own mark on how I approach leadership. There's the "coach" style, where a leader guides and motivates their team, and the "visionary" who's always looking ahead and inspiring others. Then there's the "servant" leader, who prioritizes the needs of the team, and the "diplomatic" leader, skilled in handling different viewpoints. There are so many different styles to list and each style has influenced me in different ways.

For instance, observing a purely "coaching" leader made me appreciate the value of encouragement, but I also saw how it could limit adaptability. A "visionary" leader's enthusiasm is contagious, but it can sometimes overlook the nitty-gritty details. These lessons have shaped my own leadership style, which is a blend of these approaches. I adapt based on the situation—listening intently during team meetings to foster an open environment and then switching gears to hands-on support when it's time to execute tasks.

## Embracing Your Authenticity

Embracing authenticity has been a key theme in my leadership journey. When I think about the kind of leader I want to be, I'm reminded of those who left a positive impact on me. They were genuine and didn't shy away from showing their personality. They weren't afraid to be themselves, and that made the work environment more relatable and comfortable.

Drawing from this, I encourage my team to embrace their individuality. I want them to know that it's okay to be themselves at work. When you're authentic, it builds trust and makes others feel at ease. This doesn't mean being rigid—it's about staying true to your core values while being adaptable to different situations.

My experiences with various leadership styles have shown me the power of authenticity. It's not just a buzzword; it's a guiding principle that fosters a culture of respect, openness, and collaboration. By being authentic, you create a leadership style that's uniquely yours, and that's where the magic happens. Your team members will recognize and appreciate it, and they'll feel more motivated and connected. So, as we continue exploring the art of crafting a leadership style, remember that being yourself is the best way to inspire and lead others.

## Being a Female Leader Behind the Scenes: Thriving in the Operations Role

Being a female leader behind the scenes isn't just a role I step into—it's where I genuinely come alive. While some people flourish in the spotlight, I've discovered that my true power and contributions shine brightest when I'm orchestrating things from behind the scenes.

What truly sets me apart as a leader is the sheer joy I find in being behind the curtain. There's an unmistakable sense of fulfillment and purpose that accompanies the meticulous work of ensuring everything runs like a well-oiled machine. I've always been drawn to the mechanics of an operation—the careful planning, the intricate coordination, and the precision of execution. While the stage is where the final act takes place, it's behind the scenes where the real magic is woven, piece by piece.

This preference for the operations side isn't just about comfort—it's about tapping into my strengths. I've come to realize that I'm at my best as a leader when I'm not in the limelight. It's not about avoiding attention; it's about embracing a role that lets me leverage my skills and expertise in the most impactful way. I've found that I can truly focus on the nitty-gritty details, anticipate potential roadblocks, and streamline processes when I'm not pulled in different directions by the demands of being in front of a camera or in the public eye.

What's truly intriguing is that this inclination towards leading behind the scenes doesn't dilute the impact of my leadership—it amplifies it. While my approach might not always command the same immediate attention as a charismatic leader in the spotlight, its influence is deeply felt in the results we achieve. The teams I've had the privilege of working with have experienced a remarkable sense of unity and purpose that emanates from a finely tuned operation.

## Embracing Leadership: Your Journey, Your Symphony

Embracing your leadership journey and crafting your unique symphony involves a deliberate and introspective process. Let's break it down into actionable steps:

### Step 1: Self-Reflection and Awareness

1. Explore Your Values: Take time to identify your core values and beliefs. What drives you? What do you stand for? Your values will serve as the foundation of your leadership style.

2. Assess Your Strengths: Recognize your strengths and areas where you excel. Are you a natural motivator, a strategic thinker, a problem solver, or a skilled communicator? Understanding your strengths will help you harness them in your leadership approach.

## Step 2: Learn from Others

1. Study Different Styles: Familiarize yourself with various leadership styles, such as coaching, visionary, diplomatic, and servant leadership. Observe leaders you admire and identify elements you resonate with.

2. Extract Lessons: Reflect on the experiences you've had with different leadership styles. What worked well? What could be improved? Extract valuable lessons from both positive and negative encounters.

## Step 3: Define Your Authentic Leadership

1. Embrace Your Authenticity: Understand that authenticity is your greatest asset. Embrace your true self, quirks and all. Authentic leaders are relatable and build stronger connections with their teams.

2. Identify Your Niche: Reflect on where you feel most empowered and effective. Do you shine as a mentor, a visionary, a mediator, or a hands-on supporter? Your niche is where your leadership truly comes alive.

## Step 4: Cultivate Adaptive Leadership

1. Blend Styles: Combine elements of different leadership styles that resonate with you. Adapt your approach based on the situation—sometimes, a coaching style might be needed, while other times, a diplomatic approach might be more appropriate.

2. Effective Communication: Develop strong communication skills to convey your vision, expectations, and support to your team. Listen actively and create an open dialogue where ideas flow freely.

## Step 5: Lead with Impact

1. Empower and Elevate: As a leader, your role is to empower your team, elevate their skills, and create an environment where they can thrive. Provide opportunities for growth and encourage their unique contributions.

2. Practice Trust and Transparency: Establish trust by being transparent about your intentions, decisions, and challenges. Trust is the cornerstone of strong leadership.

3. Continuous Learning: Commit to lifelong learning and growth. Seek feedback, attend workshops, read books, and learn from both successes and failures.

## Step 6: Inspire Others

1. Share Your Journey: Share your leadership journey with your team. Be open about your experiences, challenges, and growth. Your authenticity will inspire others to embrace their own paths.

2. Encourage Individuality: Create an inclusive environment where team members feel safe to be themselves. Encourage them to embrace their strengths, ideas, and authentic selves.

3. Set the Tone: Lead by example. Your actions, attitude, and approach will set the tone for the entire team.

## Step 7: Keep Striving

1. Set Ambitious Goals: Continuously challenge yourself and your team to set ambitious goals. Strive for excellence and encourage a culture of continuous improvement.

2. Celebrate Progress: Celebrate milestones and achievements along the way. Recognize and appreciate the hard work and dedication of your team.

Embracing your leadership journey and crafting your unique symphony is an ongoing process. It requires self-awareness, adaptability, and a genuine commitment to growth. As you step into your role as a leader, remember that your symphony is a work in progress—a masterpiece that reflects your values, experiences, and aspirations, and leaves a lasting impact on those you lead.

## Alexa Elbrader

https://facebook.com/lexi.r.elbrader
https://www.instagram.com/growthrugratitude_lex/
https://www.tiktok.com/@growthrugratitude_lex
https://www.myxyngular.com/en/lexirelbrader/

"Know Your Worth" is more than just a quote for Lexi Elbrader; it's a guiding principle that has shaped her life and career. From a young age, she embraced her entrepreneurial spirit, setting high standards for herself personally and professionally. Her dream has always been to wake up every day passionate about her work, and have the time and financial freedom to travel often, all while being led by faith and gratitude.

Having battled chronic illness for two decades, this often left her feeling like she was drowning in an abyss of uncertainty. However, this challenging experience has given her a unique insight into the depths of human suffering. With an MS in Clinical Psychology, Lexi has applied her education and life experiences while harnessing her empathy and understanding to help others facing similar struggles. Her life's mission is to empower individuals to persevere and emerge stronger than ever before.

# UNCOVERING THE TRUTH - A HEALING JOURNEY BEYOND BIG PHARMA

By Alexa Elbrader

Is your vision for life bigger than what surrounds you? Do you have a longing to change the world around you and within you? Advocating for the well-being of both myself and others has been the driving force behind every decision I've made, including the career path I've chosen. I have a unique story, and I'm blessed to have found a company that allows me to tell that story in a way that extends more than just hope to others. What might seem like a series of unfortunate setbacks has, in reality, set the stage for an opportunity that allowed me to tap into a $152 billion industry with groundbreaking products and a way to empower others to do the same.

But first, before I share more about this extraordinary business opportunity that came my way, a bit about my story and what led me here.

My journey to health and healing has been anything but easy; in fact, the enthusiasm I have for wellness, while beautiful and life-giving, has had rather grim origins. At the age of 16, I received the diagnoses of major depressive disorder and chronic Epstein-Barr virus. Over the course of the next two decades, I tried more than 15 different antidepressants, visited countless doctors, and spent a small fortune on supplements and lab testing–all to no avail. Although I had two diagnoses, I always knew there was more going on beneath the murky waters of my health. No matter how many methods I tried or how much I begged for answers and relief, I was left aimlessly drifting in a dark sea of confusion and doubt.

For what felt like an eternity, I lived in survival mode, battling the relentless trio of debilitating fatigue, chronic illness, and overwhelming financial stress. As time wore on, my health steadily declined, each passing day chipping away at my strength. I convinced myself that the harsh truth of my existence would be characterized by illness, despair, exhaustion, and the crushing feeling that I would miss out on life's best moments.

During these challenging times, I was reminded of my mother's words of wisdom–she always told me that each of us has a cross to carry in this life, and while suffering is inevitable, there is always hope. Even in the darkest moments when my hope was hanging by a thread and I wasn't sure if I'd make it out alive, my faith remained unshakeable. By some miracle, I was able to carry on.

Upon obtaining my Master's Degree in Clinical Psychology, I successfully secured my dream job as a Crisis Hospital Therapist at a Children's Psychiatric Hospital. However, after only two years into this rewarding and highly demanding profession, I was compelled to resign and confront the harsh reality of my declining health. This was a terrifying step for me. Finding a balance between prioritizing my health and pursuing my passion was crucial. Despite the uncertainties, I decided to take the leap of faith anyway.

Fast forward two and a half years to a defining moment in my journey –a moment that shattered my belief in the very system that I had trusted for so long. One ordinary day, the pain became more than I could bear. I decided to admit myself into the ER in hopes of finally finding some answers. Sadly, this hospital trip would be my first and last.

Three hours passed as I lay in the hospital bed, overwhelmed by how utterly lifeless I felt. As the doctor entered the room, the verdict sounded all too familiar.

"You're having an anxiety attack," she said flatly.

Her words left a pit in my stomach and only added to the lifelessness I already felt. There's something acutely painful about continuously having your symptoms minimized and pain trivialized.

The crushing grief that enveloped me in that moment led to a realization—I was fighting a battle that Big Pharma could never truly understand or cure. Empathy flooded my heart as I thought about the countless others who were facing similar situations. Did they know how to advocate for themselves? Did they know how to tune out the thousands of voices of medical experts and listen to what their bodies were trying to tell them?

The prospect that other people–people like me–are feeling lost and misunderstood ignited a fire in my heart. This defining moment became a catalyst for change within me. I was compelled to start a mission of self-healing and simultaneously become a guide for others lost in the same sea of confusion and doubt.

As I began my journey toward true healing, I came to learn that a significant portion of the autoimmune community finds relief and answers through word of mouth, and, believe it or not, autoimmunity-related Facebook support groups. I was astounded that a Facebook group comprised of ordinary people was more enlightening than 15 years' worth of doctors and experts! The insight and comfort I received from the digital community renewed my spirit in ways the pharmaceutical industry never had before.

For the first time in my life, I felt like my story was heard–really heard. Not only did I feel profoundly understood, but I felt like I had an actual direction to pursue and guidance to support me along the way.

Due to all the symptoms I had experienced over the years, this virtual community informed me that my doctor should have referred me to a number of different specialists including naturopaths, rheumatologists, sleep specialists, and functional medicine doctors, none of which I even knew existed. How was it possible that my doctor never thought to inform me of such basic health principles but a Facebook community did? Instead of looking for the root cause of my illness, he wrote me band-aid cover-up prescriptions for Adderall.

It was only because of these support groups that I realized just how completely the medical industry had failed me. Their conventional treatments and pharmaceutical approaches left me no better than before. Don't get me wrong–traditional medicine can be successful for some, but it falls massively short when it comes to treating chronic illnesses and most forms of disease. Which means people don't find true healing, and isn't that what we're all desperately searching for?

My decision to cut ties with Big Pharma and forge my own path away from traditional medicine and toward true wellness was the beginning of genuine healing. It was during this journey that I unearthed the real culprit behind the pain and suffering that had plagued me for decades: I had Lyme disease–a bacterial disease that is characterized by a range of symptoms including fatigue, joint pain, flu symptoms, headaches and weakness, among many other symptoms. If left untreated, it can lead to more severe complications affecting the heart and nervous system, to name a few.

This time, I wasn't so eager to run back to my old doctors. In fact, I avoided them at all costs. Instead, I ventured into a world of physicians and specialists who operated outside of Big Pharma. As I met with different experts, one common truth came to light: I needed to get to the root cause of my issues by healing my gut.

At 28 years old, gut health was a new concept for me, and I would be lying if I said I wasn't skeptical. What in the world was gut health? Was it actually going to solve my problems? I was debilitatingly fatigued. So how exactly was focusing on my gut going to fix that, along with the countless additional symptoms I experienced on a daily basis?

However, I soon discovered that these specialists were echoing the wisdom of Hippocrates, who famously stated that "all disease begins in the gut." So I took a leap of faith, committed to taking on the task of healing my gut, and quickly came to learn that if all disease begins in the gut, healing has to start there, too. Under the guidance of my functional medicine doctor at the time, I began a regimen of supplements aimed at healing my gut. Three months passed with no noticeable changes.

That's when a friend introduced me to the Gut Collective, a line of products designed to promote gut healing and overall mind-body health. Within just three days, these products proved to be life-altering for me, embodying everything I had come to learn about taking a root cause approach to healing. My gut was finally beginning to heal. Within a month, the visible impact was remarkable as I shed eight pounds of stubborn weight that had been clinging to my gut area. Moreover, inches disappeared from my waistline. Not only did I experience physical changes, but I also noticed increased mental clarity, improved moods, and newfound overall well-being, all serving as a compelling testament to the profound effectiveness of gut healing. As a result of their effectiveness, it was a natural choice for me to become an X-Brand partner for Xyngular - a company that I knew I had to share with the world.

For me, there were two main reasons that I was convinced I had found the best of the best with the Gut Collective product line. First, it was very apparent that they worked with my body due to the rapid improvement I experienced. Second, I had complete trust in the biochemist who was behind creating the Gut Collective products, Chanelle Cozette.

When considering becoming an X-Brand partner, it was crucial for me to ensure that the Gut Collective products aligned with my principles of using natural, high-quality, and reliable sources. As I heard more about Chanelle's story, I discovered that she had experienced a lot of the same autoimmune issues I was facing. She intimately understood the challenges of dealing with fatigue, depression, acne, hormonal imbalances, stubborn weight gain, joint pain, and other challenging symptoms. Unable to find a solution through traditional medicine, she took matters into her own hands and created the Gut Collective product line.

The Gut Collective products, which worked diligently to restore balance within my body, became the answer I had been searching for all along. Their synergistic properties function to restore balance within our microbiome, the key to 70% of our health and healing, which is intricately linked to our immune system. Moreover, our gut produces approximately 95% of the body's serotonin—the hormone that governs happiness, desire, and sleep. Astonishingly, the gut serves as the control center for our entire body, influencing cravings, mental wellness, energy levels, metabolism, digestion, hormonal regulation, and all aspects of our well-being. It's no exaggeration to say that the gut operates as our second brain, having formed even before our physical bodies in the womb!

Now, two years into my gut healing journey, I'm more confident than ever that traditional medicine led me astray. I'd be willing to bet there are many others out there who have also experienced firsthand the deficits and shortcomings of Big Pharma.

The truth is, modern society has distanced us from our inherent human nature. We have been conditioned to trust and follow doctors unquestioningly, we're told that band-aid cover-ups are our only options, and we blindly believe that feeling unwell is just part of the human experience. Simply put, that's just not true. In fact, healing is a lot simpler than what we've been led to believe. In our fast-paced world, our daily consumption often consists of processed and nutritionally deficient foods that set us on a path toward cancer, disease, inflammation, and pain. Unfortunately, the pharmaceutical industry's "quick fix" solutions only perpetuate this catastrophic cycle.

According to an article from Stanford University School of Medicine, "Doctors have historically received almost no nutritional training, which limits their ability to effectively talk to patients about it. During four years of medical school, most students spend fewer than 20 hours on nutrition. That's completely disproportionate to its health benefits for patients." Yes, you read that correctly. Doctors are not nutritional experts, but shouldn't they be? After all, food is what powers our bodies; it's what makes us able to get up and function (or not function). And yet doctors aren't trained to understand how nutrition affects us. Instead, they're trained to write prescriptions that don't address the root cause of issues. This doesn't make sense because you can't expect a bandaid to heal a bullet hole, can you?

I think this is something people really need to wake up and realize. Our bodies are not designed to perpetually run on empty. We need holistic, nourishing foods as well as rest, connection with nature, and life-giving relationships. Body, soul, and mind must align for true health to be possible. Neglecting these essential aspects of life inhibits our healing potential. And if doctors are here to heal us, then why are they neglecting the very things that lead to healing?

Hippocrates is widely known as the father of medicine, and for good reason. He believed that "the greatest medicine of all is teaching people how not to need it." In other words, the goal of medicine should be to get people to a place where they no longer need it. Once someone no longer depends on medication, that's when it becomes clear they've achieved healing.

I now know without a doubt that true healing begins with gut health.

A balanced gut sets off a chain reaction, which brings the body into harmonious alignment. However, not all gut health products are created equally. The Gut Collective's superior products are designed to literally change your body from the inside out. You will see positive changes, feel pain and fatigue subside, and watch your body age in reverse when you commit to the Gut Collective. I can assure you it's not an exaggeration to say that your body, physically and mentally, will undergo a remarkable transformation once you heal your gut. And I think everyone deserves to feel and look their very best in this one life we have to live.

Within this transformative company, I discovered a vision for a brighter future. I aspire to enable others to embrace a comprehensive approach to wellness. I aim to create a safe haven where the hopeless find hope, the misunderstood find understanding, the disconnected feel connected, and the unheard find their voice. My studies, along with my own struggles, have cultivated empathy and enabled me to connect with others on a profound level. Whether through personal interactions or community initiatives, my goal is to create a ripple effect of positive change, empowering others to take control of their health and heal from within.

It brings me joy to know that these aspirations of mine are entirely possible because of what being an X-brand partner means. When you join the team, here are a few of the incredible benefits you can expect:

- A simple business structure with built-in flexibility. Sign up, share, and earn daily pay all while setting your own schedule. Bonus: we create the marketing material and provide you with your own website!

- A positive and inclusive work environment that prioritizes unity over competition.

- A supply of natural plant-based, award-winning supplements that have a 94% success rate.

- A life of adventure–think world travel and 5-star resort accommodations for two in places like Jamaica, Dubai, Europe, etc.

- A role in one of the fastest growing, well-established industries (already at $151.9 BILLION and projected to grow by 8% every year). It's an industry that will never go out of style because wellness will always be needed in our lives.

- A willable income, meaning the business you work hard to build can be passed down to those who come after you.

As someone who once faced the darkness of hopelessness and uncertainty of survival, the thought of others experiencing such despair is what motivates me to succeed. As I stand tall today, I see a future where individuals embrace the power of self-healing, find solace in a supportive community, and embark on a transformative journey toward health and happiness. This is my mission, my purpose, and my commitment—to be a beacon of hope and change in the lives of those who seek relief and recovery, whether that be physically, mentally, or financially. Together, we will embrace the power of self-healing and cultivate a shared sense of purpose, illuminating the path towards brighter days and a more fulfilling life.

## Sarah Whyte

CEO of Sarah L. Whyte Consulting

https://www.linkedin.com/in/sarahlwhyte/
https://www.facebook.com/iamsarahlwhyte/
https://www.instagram.com/iamsarahlwhyte
www.sarahlwhyte.com
www.bloatnomore.com

Sarah Whyte is the CEO of SolisLabs, Bloat No More, and Sarah L. Whyte Consulting. All are targeted to help others achieve success in their health and wellness. She has a Bachelor of Science (B.S.) focused in Psychology/Family Therapy from Ohio State University and 12 years of experience in the Nutraceutical Industry.

Through her professional and personal experiences, Sarah knew she was born to motivate others to live healthy and inspiring lives while making an impact on the world. Whether it's through masterminds, retreats, brand classes, or personal connections, she is constantly looking for a new way to inspire others beyond their limits of expectations.

When Sarah is not working on inciting positive changes in the worlds of others, you can find her traveling, gardening, fly fishing, and dancing in the kitchen. Sarah is truly for the people and her genuineness is evident in her words, thoughts, and actions.

# I CHOOSE TO BELIEVE

By Sarah Whyte

Our thoughts are powerful catalysts for the way we view ourselves, the world, and others, but how can we use this power for good and transform our thoughts into ones that will incite positivity and productivity? We must choose to believe. At times, we create statements in our minds that are untrue and can damage our perspective, but with the right mindset we can transform these thoughts into what I like to call "I choose to believe" statements.

In order to create these statements, you must first compile a list of 30 thoughts that are considered belief-bind statements – statements in which you acquaint one situation with another. For example, stating, "The more I say no to people, the less likely they are to want to spend time with me," is considered a belief-bind statement. After compiling a list of 30 belief-bind statements, I now want you to transform them into "I choose to believe statements". For the example above the belief statement could transform into, "I choose to believe that setting boundaries within my relationship will foster healthier and stronger connections with my loved ones." This change in perspective of our own thoughts will make all the difference in the way we hold ourselves up and the respect we demand for ourselves.

My journey to believing in myself and getting where I am today – like most others – was not an easy feat. My home life consisted of a single-family trailer park home in Reynoldsburg, Ohio. Due to my upbringing, children at school would taunt me and claim I would never amount to anything past my circumstances. Moments such as those are turning points in one's life; we can choose to allow them to dig their way into our skin and never leave, or we can use them as motivators for our own success. I chose the latter.

In December 2011, I became the first person in my family to graduate from college. I attended The Ohio State University and got a Bachelor of Science (B.S.) in Psychology/Family Therapy. Once college was behind me, I looked ahead toward the next part of my adventure in the sunny state of California. At the time, I had no set plans in mind, but I knew one thing for certain: whatever project I decided to take on, I was going to be the boss.

Due to my upbringing, I was introduced to the working world at the early age of thirteen years old. I worked through all the classic run-of-the-mill jobs, some were more brutal than others, but above all, they all taught me the importance of a hard work ethic. The most intentional way to live is to take every experience and turn it into something worthwhile for your own growth and individuality. The skills I developed throughout these several jobs helped support me well into my move to California.

No one can ever really prepare you for the challenges you face when you set off on your own. Finding your footing can be tedious, but it is all about the adventure. In the early part of my time in California, I was introduced to the dietary supplement industry and I immediately knew it was something I could see myself having a larger stake in. I have always prioritized health and wellness in my own life, and it was wonderful to find an industry in which I had the capacity to now share that love with others. After gaining some insight into the industry, I decided it was time I made my dreams a reality. I left my comfortable six-figure job in hopes of fueling that fire for business I had inside of me. And so, my first company was born – SolisLabs a supplement manufacturing company.

As someone with a background in family therapy, building a business from the ground up is not something I was even remotely familiar with. It took time, effort, patience, and dedication. I grinded day in and day out. My first year in the business world I lived completely off of my savings, and my yearly total earnings came out to a little under $8k. I had to supplement my income by becoming an Uber driver just to make ends meet, but eventually – by the third year of opening SolisLabs – we had come to a place of success and stability. Today, SolisLabs Supplement Manufacturing Company is nine years strong, and I could not be more proud of its history, the relationships I have created with other manufacturers, and the skills I have acquired.

While SolisLabs was created from a place of passion for wellness and a drive for the world of business, my next company – Bloat No More – was fostered by a very personal experience. The loss of my father, John. In 2017, I got a call that changed my life forever. It was my stepmother telling me that my father was being admitted to a hospital and that the doctors had found several lesions on his spleen and a large mass on his liver. It is moments such as this one in which your life truly does change forever. I went to spend time with my father in his final days, and lost him to cancer in September of 2017.

Losing my father was a devastating yet transformative experience. I have always been someone who wants their work to help others, but losing my father sparked that passion beyond any limits. Losing him made me realize that the world needs more health awareness, and I was going to be the one to inspire it. At the time, I was struggling with my own gut health issues, so creating a supplement that would transform people's gut and overall health felt like the perfect move.

I strove to build a platform that provides quality products and resources to all, while creating a genuine community that uplifts one another in our health and wellness endeavors. My main focus was on creating an environment where every woman feels heard, understood, and empowered in her gut health journey and beyond. Bloat No More stands for three authentic values: empathy, quality, and empowerment.

Thanks to my work, I wake up each morning with the feeling of immense gratitude that I am able to make a positive impact in our lives. It is my customers' stories of transformation, newfound confidence, and joy in their health that fuel my passion for this mission. I am able to reaffirm my belief in sisterhood whenever I see women supporting each other with my business as the catalyst.

Having successfully created and built two different businesses from the ground up, I next felt compelled to share all I had learned and continue to learn about business with the world. In 2021, I created my personal brand to help entrepreneurs launch and scale their supplements brands with ease. I wanted to share the wealth of knowledge I have acquired with my fellow aspiring entrepreneurs. Through this work, I have helped several supplements brands scale from nothing to six and seven-figure incomes.

As with any business entrepreneur, you may be wondering "what's next"? The fire never stops burning, and it is with that fire that I launched my first book called *Hey You…Be Your Authentic Self*. With this book, I hope to guide women on a path toward a purposeful life. I want women to finish my book feeling fully motivated, on fire, and ready to embody the woman she is meant to be. Along with my book, I have curated a mastermind called the Soul Fam Inner Circle Mastermind in which we dive deeper into moving beyond past fears and leading life with confidence.

One of my biggest motivations stems from watching others succeed and live the life they deserve. My hope is that readers of my book and customers of my companies feel that in every sector of my work. Guiding women to see their beauty and greatest potential only helps to make me more aligned with my mission. All of my work — whether it be my businesses or personal development support — is created with the best intentions for others in mind.

To truly step into one's authentic power is to know oneself. Don't just take my word for it, get yourself a copy of *Hey You... Be Your Authentic Self* today and get started in achieving all that you desire.

Many of us have great ideas, but are lost on where to begin. I am here to tell you that you are capable of all that you envision for yourself. It takes dedication and a consistent amount of small steps to reach the bigger picture.

Nothing is built in a day, but choosing to have faith in yourself and your dreams is going to be the first step toward your ideal reality. We are all capable of achieving our wildest dreams; all you have to do is *choose to believe*. Are you ready to join me on the journey towards our most coveted passions?

## Christi Pratte

Founder of Ghost Girl & HustlePretty.Co
Writer

https://www.linkedin.com/in/christi-pratte-1207b718b
https://www.facebook.com/christi.pratte.3?mibextid=LQQJ4d
https://www.instagram.com/christipratte/
https://www.hustlepretty.co/
https://www.ghostgirlwriting.com/

Christi is the founder of HustlePretty.Co and Ghost Girl. After working seven years as a kindergarten teacher, kickboxing instructor, barista, waitress, and tutor, she began exploring her love for writing by blogging. She quickly gained global readership, which opened the invitation to contribute to leading women's empowerment magazines. Since 2019, she has contributed over 80 articles. Christi rebranded her blog into HustlePretty.Co, which displays articles and interviews on the topics of self-love, resiliency, and business. She started her writing service, Ghost Girl, in 2020 to amplify women's voices and personal brands through creative copywriting. She has had the honor of serving numerous female entrepreneurs including public figures, bestselling authors, and industry thought leaders. Christi is passionate about using the power of the pen as a modality for women to share their stories and rise to their fullest potential, all while leading the way for the next woman.

# PASSION, A PEN, AND THE COLLECTED WISDOM OF MY PAST

By Christi Pratte

They say from the hardest falls come the greatest rises, and now I see why.

For the majority of my twenties I was what you would call a "hustler". For seven years I was simultaneously working 4+ jobs. All of which I loved.

Out of college, I was fortunate enough to be offered the opportunity to initiate a kindergarten program at a small private school. I worked closely with my boss and colleagues to create a curriculum from scratch. My boss was a strong, female leader who was passionate about redefining education to put students first. She was warm and loving with a beautiful sense of humor. Her effortless confidence taught me the power of following your heart and fighting for a vision that sometimes only *you* can see. With her leadership in tandem with an intimate team of teachers who became some of my closest friends, we were able to watch the vision flourish in our school. Our child-centered approach to education uniquely integrated academics with play-based learning that fostered each child's curiosity. This was every rookie teacher's dream come true. The industry is competitive, so finding a job upon graduation is rare, never mind finding a perfectly aligned fit. As amazing as the endeavor was, I accepted it knowing that the growth may be slow, as all startups tend to be. In that first year, we had the enrollment to only cover a half-day program. Little did I know that what started out as a quest to close the gap in my income and cover my bills would turn into the map that led me to where I am today.

I didn't just pick up one new job, I picked up three. My sister's roommate from college, whom I had met and adored over the years, opened up a quaint little coffee shop down the street. Within the first year that she opened the doors, I submitted my application and was thrilled to be welcomed into the cafe family as a barista. The owner was a young, business-savvy trailblazer and well ahead of her time for local female entrepreneurship. She led with integrity and a true love for the city. I watched as her efforts cultivated a close-knit community and sparked a vibrancy that was previously missing in the concrete chaos. Over the next decade, other young entrepreneurs began to follow in her footsteps by opening up their own dreams along the strip. Wide-eyed, I found this energy magnetic. I loved meeting all the blossoming entrepreneurs, learning their stories, and hearing what inspired them to take the road less traveled.

Now that I had secured my caffeine fix, I continued my pursuit. Eventually I stumbled upon a winery that had recently opened in a neighboring town. The second I walked through the grandiose double doors I was captivated by the luxurious ambiance. The aromatic atmosphere pulled me in, but if I'm honest, my heart preceded me. I was hired on the spot as a server. I'll never forget how on my first shift the owner and winemaker, who was a charismatic woman, the type of person who makes everybody feel like somebody, came up and introduced herself with a bright smile. I watched as she confidently circulated the bistro in a similar fashion, greeting all those who came to dine. While I'm certain she had a calendar busting at the seams, she always took the time to show her guests around, share her latest concoctions, and make them feel like they had arrived home. She genuinely cared about her team, staff, and patrons and it was felt. Over the years I deeply appreciated her ability to balance the titles of mother, wife, businesswoman, and winemaker. She went on to successfully open up numerous locations and develop a booming wedding venue. And yet she would still be there, front row, for her sons' soccer games. She would always say "I'm a mother first." I admired her values and her exceptional generosity.

But let me take you back before that. After all, what would this chapter be without a love story, right? It was in high school that I encountered my first true love — kickboxing. As an active teen and committed athlete, I was constantly bouncing in and out of fitness classes. I tried it all on for size – Zumba, spinning, pilates, barre, yoga, and everything in between. But they all felt like…work. That was until I discovered kickboxing and the magic of martial arts. For the first time, exercise didn't just feel physical. It provided a holistic experience of mental, physical, and emotional release. I was hooked. I never knew punching heavyweight bags could feel like meditation, but it did. One class a week quickly turned into three, then five, then I was pretty much living at the dojo. The feeling never faded like it did with other exercise classes. Eventually the sensei approached me about becoming an instructor to replace one of the senior instructors who would be leaving the dojo soon. She was a small but mighty type of woman. Fiery, no BS, and at the same time a total sweetheart. Her expertise was unmatched and she took me under her wing to teach me all the necessary skills to accelerate my practice to the next level. As we were training, a new skill set presented itself – mental strength. I realized how limiting my own thoughts and beliefs were, from not feeling good enough and doubting my abilities to being overly critical of my efforts. Her words were just as powerful as her punches, and she had a way of empowering my confidence. Because of her tough love, I took on my first class solo and filled the room with 20+ badass women. At that moment I realized this wasn't about me at all, it was about THEM. And just like that, the doubts disappeared.

As I continued to teach classes at multiple gyms around the city, I had the honor of witnessing the transformation my students underwent. They would come through the doors with a vanity-based goal (as all of us ladies find ourselves guilty of from time to time) — to get six-pack abs, more toned arms, or lessen the appearance of cellulite. But as they became addicted to the craft just as I had, their goals changed. They developed physical strength, but more importantly mental strength. I saw that these women became more empowered in their everyday lives thanks to the time they spent on the mats. They were telling me about life-changing events that were unfolding like finding the courage to leave toxic relationships, asking their boss for a raise, and no longer hiding from cameras because they hated the way they looked. The internal shifts were seismic. Hearing these stories sparked my passion to speak to the healing powers of true self-love, empowerment, and confidence.

As time moved forward, many people asked me how I did it all without burning out. My simple answer was passion. When you're passionate about what you're doing, the work hits differently. I believe burnout only comes when we're out of alignment, have lost the intrinsic reward of fulfilling our purpose, or have hit a growth cap and are ready for something different. As I kept receiving questions about my lifestyle, I decided to start a blog to share my thoughts. I infused my love for kickboxing and my driving force of passion to launch my first blog – The Passion Warrior Project.

I'd type away during all my "free time." Those 20 minutes between jobs, at 4AM, and sometimes when I'd get home from my last shift around midnight. My blog became my sanctuary. I loved having a place to go to indulge my creativity, process life, and take others along with me. Truthfully, I didn't think anyone else was even reading until I logged into my analytics app to see that my corner of cyberspace had reached the eyes of over 20 countries.

While it all felt like a fairytale about to unfold, that growth cap found me. As someone who believed she was immune to burnout, I found myself gripped by its contagion. Writing became my new obsession. I wanted to write all the time. As I got my morning coffee, I dreamed of what it would be like to sit at the cafe for the rest of the day and get lost in my keys.

All of a sudden the everyday work felt like work. And that's not to say I loved it any less, it still had my heart. But my heart was beating for more. Because of this I was crawling my way through. Life got heavier and heavier, perhaps even a little suffocating. I knew I should take the leap into a writing career, but had no idea how or where to start. So I pushed the idea away and ignored its persistent calls.

They say when you don't acknowledge the lion within, its roars will become louder. What you resist, persists. Well, that's exactly what happened. By spinning my wheels and not taking action on what I intuitively knew to be my purpose, I was suddenly face-to-face with a tragic situation that halted me dead in my tracks. Things certainly got louder before they simmered to silence, and I'm grateful they did because if that scenario never happened, I would have never made the move for myself. It was the pattern interrupt I desperately needed.

This is what they call divine intervention. But at the time it felt like the lowest of lows. I couldn't see the next step. I had been completely humbled and thrown to my knees, and for the first time in a long time, I was forced to slow down and be free of distraction. I drew closer to my family, friends, and community who showed me unconditional love and support. I knew I had two options — to stay down or to stand up. They believed in me, and it was time to believe in me too. I chose to alchemize this dark moment of my life into a launchpad for self-discovery. I dove headfirst into every personal development book I could get my hands on. I invited others on the journey with me, opening up a virtual book club where over 500 women joined in on the adventure of embracing self-empowerment.

During this time, my writing intensified. I was feverishly writing article after article. With a blog to my name, I started pitching myself to write for bigger platforms that I truthfully had no business pitching myself to because I had no "real" experience or degree. But I had a very real purpose that needed a place.

I was stunned by how many responses I received that were open to collaborating. With each "yes", my fear of rejection faded. These platforms became the gateway that opened up a loyal readership. Women were flooding my inbox thanking me for my work and sharing how it impacted their lives. The power of the pen was not lost on me. I knew I needed to take this to a larger level, but again – how?

As I was emerging out of this dark season, I found myself scrolling through Spotify one night when I came across the cover art of Carrie Underwood's *Cry Pretty* album. On display was a picture of Carrie with thick, black mascara tears streaming down her face but in stark contrast, the mascara streaks had glitter painted over them. I loved this symbolism of strength in weakness, grace in grit, light in dark, and the *pretty in hustle*. It spoke to my soul. That's when I rebranded The Passion Warrior Project into what is now HustlePretty.Co: a blog centered on passion, empowerment, and redefining success for women.

Still in my job flow, I by chance came across a listing on Craigslist for a copywriter position at a prestigious, multi-million dollar women's empowerment company. I scraped together my published pieces into a portfolio, polished up my resume, and audaciously applied. Again to my surprise, I was invited to an interview. Insanely nervous with a tinge of imposter syndrome lurking in the background, I showed up. "What are you even doing here?" My mind would taunt. Mid-interview I could feel myself sweating and stumbling on my words, so I stopped and said, "I don't know, but what I do know is I can do this, I want to do this!"

Long story short, they graciously took a chance on me. One week prior to the 2020 pandemic, I signed the contracts and never looked back as I gently closed the chapter to my old work life and embraced this new one.

As 2020 progressed, I noticed the undeniable need for people to speak up, share their stories, and influence change. And like many people, this pivotal moment in history had me asking the bigger question: "How can I contribute?" I truly believe we all hold special gifts unique to this time on the planet. That's when I embraced mine to open up Ghost Girl, a freelance writing service for female entrepreneurs specializing in capturing the story behind personal brands. I guess you could say the spirit of assisting female entrepreneurs and thirst for entrepreneurial energy, unbeknownst to me, had been in my blood all along. In the famous words of Steve Jobs, "You can't connect the dots looking forward, only looking backward."

Having been through what I went through, I knew the healing power of the pen and I wanted to facilitate this process for other women so they could share their voice with those who needed to hear it most. From the beginning, I was fortunate enough to find soul-sister clients. Women who were heart-centered changemakers ready to put personality to paper, infuse ink with intuition, etch emotion into emails, and articulate art through articles.

As I write this to you, I'm excited to say that I've recently taken the full entrepreneurial leap to see this vision through. With passion and a pen, plus the collected wisdom of my past experiences, I now see how each became a star in the Ghost Girl constellation.

I hope this small glimpse into my story shines inspiration into yours. Trust the process. Follow your intuition. Be fierce in the pursuit of your vision. Lead with purpose. Honor your values. Take action. Listen to your heart. Know that your unique gift is your responsibility. Stay humble. Discover how you can be of service to others. Use the dark times as your light. Embrace your evolution. Ask the better questions. Prioritize self-discovery. Rise like a phoenix. And when you do all this, the pure simplicity of your presence becomes the fueling fire behind iconic leadership…behind your legacy.

**Ilka Bee**

CEO of Nurture Beyond Baby

http://www.linkedin.com/in/nurturebeyondbaby
https://www.facebook.com/profile.php?id=100094636652595
https://www.instagram.com/nurturebeyondbaby/
www.nurturebeyondbaby.com

Ilka Bee, a 42-year-old powerhouse, transformed her life from a trapped, corporate marketing executive to an empowered entrepreneur. After a divorce, she embarked on a soul-searching journey across continents, exploring different careers. Eventually, she found her true calling in the world of birth.

For a decade, Ilka has been an advocate for empowering births outside the medical system. She has experienced the beauty of undisturbed home births three times. Currently residing in Mexico, Ilka and her husband are raising their three little ones in the serene Baja California desert.

Ilka's mission and unwavering dedication extend beyond her family as she educates and supports mothers worldwide on physiological birth and postpartum care.

She now supports couples on their journey into parenthood, specializing in that crucial first year of parenting. Focusing on helping fathers understand what their partners go through, she equips them to be the best support possible.

# BIRTH IN POWER- AWAKEN YOUR INTUITION AND RECLAIM YOUR MOTHERLY INSTINCTS

By Ilka Bee

Ladies - Let me tell you a powerful secret they're trying to keep from us:

Women have the innate wisdom to know how to birth, and babies instinctively know how to be born.

It's our species' survival instinct, encoded in our DNA.

Nature's blueprint works flawlessly if we just let it unfold without interference.

Yet, birth trauma is a daily occurrence in our Western hospitals and a sad initiation into motherhood for too many women.

"Peace on Earth begins with birth!" My late mentor, Jeannine Pavarti, used to say.

Despite her wisdom, they insist on confining childbirth to the hospital. They insist on subjecting us to countless tests and ultrasounds as if we don't already know how to grow and nurture a baby. They insist our babies are too big, our pelvises too small, or our bodies too old to birth naturally. They insist we need drugs, epidurals, and c-sections to ensure a safe birth.

When I embarked on my journey into the world of birth as a Birthkeeper, I felt an immense honor to witness the miraculous transformation into parenthood and see women tap into their extraordinary birth power.

However, the reality I encountered was far from sacred or peaceful. Fear and disconnection ruled the birth space in hospitals. Women were stripped of their power, made to feel small and incapable, and often left physically violated and emotionally shattered.

Too many times tears would stream down my face as I drove home from the hospital in the early morning hours, overwhelmed by the heartbreaking experiences and trauma it left for mother and baby.

Those moments marked the beginning of my mission: to assist mothers in birthing outside the medical system, to advocate for homebirth. And, if the time ever came for me to have children, to never subject myself to the confines of a hospital.

I vividly recall my very first client, Sarah, in California about 15 years ago. She was expecting her first baby. At our appointments, we shared laughter, hugs, and tears as we created her "dream birth" and postpartum plan. She felt prepared for what lay ahead.

One hot July morning, she texted that her water broke, and she was on her way to the hospital. I still wish to this day that my past self knew what I know now. I should have told her to relax, stay at home, and take it easy.

Most women experience contractions within 24 hours or less after their water breaks. But instead, I followed her wish to head to the hospital. There, we learned that the baby's heartbeat was strong, her blood pressure perfect. Hours passed, and still, no contractions.

She snuggled with her hubby, took walks, and climbed stairs. But no contractions started. Almost ten hours later, the doctor walked into her room. "Sarah, I think it's time we start the induction. Your body doesn't want to get this party started on its own, it seems."

I could feel the belittling in her tone and a sense of unease in my stomach. The doctor stated that hospital policy required an induction after 12 hours of a ruptured amniotic sac if contractions hadn't started. He explained that the risks of infection would be too high, and the patient surely wouldn't want to compromise her baby's health.

This was the first attempt to bully the mother out of her intuition. She had prepared for an all-natural birth. 19 hours later, Sarah was desperate, hungry, and miserable. The induction made the contractions unnaturally strong. She was unable to move freely due to monitors strapped around her belly and the IV line hooked to her hand.

The epidural provided some relief, but after five hours, she was labeled a "failure to progress." The doctor suggested considering a cesarean section due to the baby's declining heart tones. "I'm sure you're making the best decision for your baby. I'll let the anesthesiologist know to get you prepped."

The cohesion in his words was palpable. I glanced at Sarah's husband; his head sank. In the operating room, a mixture of relief and disbelief filled the air. She told me later that she felt completely overwhelmed by a range of emotions while being strapped down on the operating table. Sarah had lost control over what was happening to her body. She felt guilty for not giving her baby the chance to be born naturally. She was disappointed about the change of plans and afraid she would miss out on the initial bonding in that first sacred hour.

Forty-five minutes later, her healthy baby girl, Lia, was born, but Sarah's dream of a natural birth had been shattered.

The emotional impact of her traumatic experience lingered, with the physical scar still visible. Over the next few years, she experienced bouts of depression and self-doubt, pondering the reasons behind the event. She and her partner often argued about whether the c-section was truly necessary.

She intuitively knew it could have been prevented. She felt robbed of her birth experience and broken in her body. She wasn't heard, not by her doctor, her husband, or friends who kept telling her, "At least you have a healthy baby."

My stomach still churns every time I recount her story. I couldn't save her.

Only now, 15 years later, do I truly grasp the extent of what happened to her and the countless other women in our hospitals every single day.

Here's the critical point we must comprehend: her body didn't fail her! Rather, it was the failure of the medical system, and the hospital policy, that let her down.

It wasn't that her body couldn't initiate labor naturally. Instead, it was the impatience of the doctor who neglected to recognize that her body wasn't yet ready.

The decisions to induce, opt for an epidural, or proceed with a c-section were not the best choices. They were the only options remaining for her after enduring belittlement, bullying, and coercion during intense contractions that left her feeling utterly drained.

It was the medical system and its professionals that caused the very problems they later claimed to have saved her from.

The level of deception was truly unimaginable!

This is not just one mother's story; I have walked alongside many women since then. Sadly, far too many women innocently surrender their power to the medical system, believing that experts know best. However, pregnancy and birth are natural, seamlessly functioning processes intricately designed by nature.

Interestingly, we understand not to disturb a gorilla mother giving birth in the zoo, honoring the natural process with reverence—no medication, forced placenta extraction, or separation from her baby. Yet, for our species, we have forgotten it all. We disrupt the mother, interrupt the hormonal sequence, incessantly monitor her, and often snatch her baby away immediately.

Back to my client in California.

When Sarah's little girl turned three, she gave birth to a precious baby boy.

This time at home, in the water, surrounded by her husband and me, her Birthkeeper. It was a peaceful environment, just as she imagined.

And she was in power.

Her labor progressed naturally and she welcomed her healthy baby just seven hours after her first contractions. Her husband caught their son and gently placed him on her chest.

At that moment, time stood still.

Mother and baby locked eyes and fell in love!

There, Sarah rewrote her story.

A story of resilience, power, and healing.

It's time we reclaim trust in our bodies, intuition, and deeply ingrained female wisdom. Let's envision a future where women give birth autonomously and with sovereignty, supported by empowering individuals. A future where babies enter the world peacefully cradled in their parents' loving hands.

Nearly a decade had passed while supporting mothers when I found myself giving birth to my own child.

Throughout all three of my pregnancies, I deliberately chose to forgo medical prenatal care, embracing my own motherly intuition.

Each time, I opted for home births, with only my husband by my side. The experience was nothing short of magical! These are sacred experiences I will cherish forever. Because I was completely undisturbed, I was able to truly tune in and trust my birthing instincts.

I was mostly naked, moaning, my husband singing songs, and holding my hand through the hardest parts. It was incredibly peaceful and without a rush. I felt powerful and supported. My children could welcome their new sibling right as they were born, and the mama could crawl back into her own bed to snuggle up with her new baby. It was a beautiful bubble of birth bliss each time.

Now, my mission is to create this "birth bliss bubble" for other mothers and families. I support, guide, and educate women who desire to birth at home, whether in the presence of a midwife or unassisted. I firmly believe in the power of undisturbed birth, the immaculate instinct of a mother, and the significance of a peaceful beginning to life. Let's remember Jeannine Pavarti's wisdom: "Peace on Earth begins with birth!"

Through years of birthwork, I've witnessed the profound influence of our birthing experience on the transformative journey of early motherhood. It's a make-or-break moment. But let's not forget, the real battle begins when the baby arrives! That's why, in my business Nurture Beyond Baby, I'm on a mission to empower parents through the daunting first year, fostering resilience and an unwavering connection as a couple. Let's conquer parenthood together!

## Andrea Mostaffa

Andrea Mostaffa Photography
Photographer

https://facebook.com/andreamostaffaphotography
https://www.instagram.com/andreamostaffaphotography/
http://www.andreamostaffa.com/

My name is Andrea Mostaffa. I'm a passionate and dedicated photographer located in Austin, Texas. With a deep understanding of the delicate balance required to meet the demands of both motherhood and a successful photography career, I bring a unique perspective to my work. My unwavering commitment drives me to capture and preserve cherished memories for families, small businesses, and individuals alike.

As a highly skilled professional, I specialize in personal branding, portraits, and family photos. I take great pride in helping small businesses stand out from the crowd by creating dynamic visuals that engage their audiences. By collaborating closely with my clients, I excel at producing content that grabs attention and propels their businesses to new heights.

With my expertise and passion for photography, I am dedicated to providing exceptional services that meet the diverse needs of my clients.

# SHADOWS AND LIGHT

### By Andrea Mostaffa

I hope my chapter finds you feeling inspired and ready to conquer the world! Allow me to share my story with you, filled with resilience, determination, and the pursuit of dreams.

My name is Andrea Mostaffa, and my journey began in the vibrant landscapes of Mexico. Hailing from a small town nestled along the southwestern Pacific coast in Michoacán and later raised in the bustling city of Colima, my roots are deeply intertwined with the rich mosaic of Mexican culture and traditions. It is within this backdrop that my story unfolds.

My parents, Gabriel and Maria, or "Rosa," as she likes to be called, were renowned entrepreneurs in the world of encyclopedias. Growing up, I was surrounded by knowledge and the beauty of storytelling. My parents' passion for exploration influenced me greatly, planting the seeds of curiosity and creativity within me. The walls of our home were adorned with shelves bursting with books, each one a gateway to new horizons and endless possibilities.

Growing up in a small beach town surrounded by family and farm animals, my childhood was incredibly ordinary, yet it was filled with a sense of untapped potential. Even though my family often moved between cities like Colima and Michoacán, one thing remained constant: my parents' unwavering determination to explore new business opportunities.

It seemed like they had a never-ending stream of entrepreneurial ideas flowing through their veins. From wine stores to restaurants and even toy stores, they fearlessly pursued every new venture that came their way.

However, life took an unexpected turn when I was just 12 years old. My parents, once inseparable partners in both business and life, made the difficult decision to part ways, leaving me and my three siblings caught in the whirlwind of their divorce and having to move to live with my grandparents. Despite the challenges that came with it, in the face of adversity, my resilience became my guiding light. With unwavering determination, I navigated the uncharted waters of shifting family dynamics and the uncertainty that loomed overhead. Together with my siblings, we leaned on each other, drawing strength from the unbreakable bond that only family can provide.

My mother, a woman who faced countless challenges to make ends meet, always fought to provide for our family. However, I saw her struggles and knew that if she stayed, my life would be no different. So, at the age of fifteen, with a heart full of dreams and determination, I made the courageous decision to move to the United States. Alone but undeterred, I embarked on a new chapter in my life, seeking new opportunities.

I embarked on an exciting adventure when I moved to Dallas, Texas. immersed in the vibrant cultural tapestry of Dallas. I've discovered a whole new world filled with opportunities, challenges, and growth!

Life in a foreign land was not without its hurdles. When I first arrived, language barriers posed a constant challenge. But you know what? I didn't let them hold me back! I saw these barriers as stepping stones towards becoming a better communicator and a more open-minded individual.

And speaking of stepping stones, let's talk about the beautiful world of cultural differences! I found myself in awe of the diverse traditions, customs, and ways of life that surrounded me. It was like stepping into a kaleidoscope of colors where every shade represented a unique story waiting to be discovered.

Following my high school years, my passion and curiosity led me down the captivating avenues of modeling, fashion, beauty, fitness, and healthcare. I perceived these endeavors as portals, opening doors to the wondrous realm of diverse cultures and offering me the opportunity to immerse myself in their captivating embrace and gain invaluable insights along the way.

My journey took an unexpected turn when fate introduced me to my incredible husband. I had already been living in Dallas for 15 years, surrounded by an incredible circle of family and friends. It was a place where memories were made and bonds were formed. However, life had another plan in store for me, and together, my husband and I embarked on an exciting voyage to Austin, Texas, eagerly awaiting the arrival of our first child.

Suddenly, I found myself at a crossroads, with a fresh start awaiting me in the mesmerizing city of Austin. But this time, I wasn't alone. I had the joyous responsibility of raising a newborn. It was both exciting and overwhelming, especially because I didn't know many people in this new place. It was during this time that I found myself at a critical junction, carefully considering the direction to pursue.

I had the opportunity to join the real estate industry, and although it was a new venture for me, I saw it as a chance for growth and exploration. Little did I know that this decision would lead me on a path of unexpected discoveries and ignited passions.

Working in the real estate industry exposed me to the extraordinary talents of remarkable photographers. Their boundless creativity, unwavering passion, and exceptional skills mesmerized me. It was at this enchanting moment that I made the courageous decision to chase my dreams and pave my own way in the realm of photography.

The decision to become a photographer wasn't an easy one. I had always enjoyed taking pictures as a hobby, capturing precious moments and freezing them in time. But turning this passion into a successful business required more than just skills behind the camera. It demanded dedication, perseverance, and a deep understanding of the art and business of photography.

I spent countless hours researching and learning about different photography techniques, studying the works of renowned photographers, and investing in top-quality equipment. I wanted to offer my clients nothing but the best, and I knew that meant constantly pushing myself to improve and innovate.

In the early days of my business, I faced numerous challenges. Building a client base from scratch was no easy task, and competition in the photography industry was fierce. But I refused to let setbacks discourage me. With each rejection or hurdle, I became more determined to prove myself and carve a niche for my brand.

I started by offering my services to friends and family, taking every opportunity to showcase my work and build a strong portfolio. Word-of-mouth referrals began to trickle in, and slowly but surely, my client base started to grow. I focused on creating a unique and personalized experience for each client, going above and beyond to capture their vision and tell their story through my lens.

As my reputation as a photographer grew, so did the demand for my services. I expanded my offerings to include weddings, engagements, portraits, and corporate events. I invested in additional equipment and, at times, an assistant to help me meet the increasing demands of my growing business. And soon, my photographs were featured in prestigious publications.

But it wasn't just about the technical aspects of photography. I realized that building meaningful connections with my clients was equally important. I took the time to understand their stories, their passions, and what they wanted to convey through their photographs. This allowed me to create images that not only captured their beauty but also reflected their personalities and emotions.

Through my photography, I discovered the power of storytelling. Each image had the ability to evoke emotions, spark memories, and transport people to a different time and place. I realized that I wasn't just capturing moments; I was creating art that would be cherished for generations to come.

As my business flourished, I also began to explore the world of entrepreneurship beyond photography. I launched an online platform where I shared my knowledge and expertise with aspiring photographers and small businesses, offering workshops, tutorials, and resources to help them navigate their own entrepreneurial journeys. I found immense joy in empowering others to pursue their passions and turn them into successful businesses.

Today, as I reflect on my journey, I am filled with gratitude for the opportunities and experiences that photography and entrepreneurship have brought into my life. They have allowed me to connect with incredible individuals, celebrate milestones, and achieve personal and professional fulfillment. Despite the challenges of my past, these days I'm happily settled in Austin, TX, with my amazing husband Mike, who is incredibly supportive. We have two wonderful daughters together, Madison and Avery, who are my everything.

I also had the opportunity to create some amazing social media groups dedicated to supporting our community.

In these groups, I aim to bring people together to make a positive impact. I organize various events that promote unity, collaboration, and connection. From networking meetings to fun outings, there is something for everyone to enjoy.

But it's not just about having a good time; it's about creating lasting friendships and giving back to our community. I believe that by working together, we can achieve great things. These groups not only provide a platform for us to connect and grow but will also serve as a reminder of the power of unity.

I wanted to share my story with you to inspire you to follow your dreams, no matter how big or small they may be. Life is too short to settle for anything less than what truly makes your soul come alive. Embrace your passions, take risks, and believe in yourself. Only then can you truly lead a life filled with joy and purpose.

Andrea Mostaffa

## Elizabeth Valle

Little Liz Things
Digital Marketer and Mentor

https://www.facebook.com/little.liz.things
https://www.instagram.com/little.liz.things/
https://littlelizthings.com/

Elizabeth is a first-generation Chicana who grew up in a migrant and low-income family. This has motivated her to reach her goals and start her own business. She has her BA in Sociology and MA in Human Services.

Now, she is a mentor, social worker, advisor, and, of course, mom! She is helping other moms achieve their goals and start their own businesses!

# THE POWER OF A MOTHER'S LOVE: MY DRIVING FORCE

By Elizabeth Valle

When I reflect on why I pursued entrepreneurship and constantly strive for self-improvement, one person stands out above the rest - my mother, or as I lovingly call her, "amá." My mother was born in Mexico and barely completed the fifth grade in order to support her family financially. She married my father at the age of 18, relocated to the United States, and had my sister by the age of 19. I arrived soon after, followed by my brother four years later. My mother was a stay-at-home mom with a few odd jobs in factories and as a babysitter here and there, but she never needed to work because my father was a truck driver and sole provider. Despite only speaking Spanish, my mother managed to teach us all English and even taught her friends how to drive. Although my mother was born and raised in Mexico, she had many shortcomings in Spanish as well. She was very limited in her grammar, and I later realized that she was limited in her vocabulary as well, none of which was her fault. I noticed this when we had to translate documents for school registrations, bills, and even medical documents. Despite these shortcomings, amá never let them deter her from enjoying life. My mother is the type of person who wears her heart on her sleeve, loves to laugh, and remembers the small details while still making sure you are fed. My mother's resilience and determination in the face of obstacles continue to inspire me to this day.

Despite all of the wonderful things my mother did, I saw her through a different lens. I saw her as someone I didn't want to be and as a lesson in what I wanted in the future. Because my mother could not speak or read English, I made it a priority to learn both English and Spanish as quickly as possible so that I would never hear someone say something and not realize it was insulting. Even though no one in my family had gone to college before, I knew I wanted to be better - not just for myself, but for her. She has been my most powerful motivation and inspiration!

Growing up as a low-income migrant, Latina, and first-generation is never easy. When I first became a mother, I quickly discovered that our society does not provide a work-life balance for moms, particularly those who wish to prioritize their children while also pursuing their job goals. My mother needed to focus on raising her children since she didn't have any other options. She lacked the necessary education and finances to achieve her objectives.

Growing up, I was taught that women should be dependent on their significant others and focus completely on raising and nurturing their children. But, in classic "middle-child" form, I've always wanted to avoid that reality. That traditional mold never quite fit me. I experienced the difficulties of parenthood and how difficult it can be to add employment to the mix amid your other commitments as soon as my son was born. The reality of integrating work with the various commitments came to light, and many more challenges arose- challenges such as childcare, putting my physical health on the back burner, and missing out on priceless milestones with my son. All of these took time, energy, and attention and it seemed almost impossible to balance. I often thought to myself., "Maybe I was meant to be like my mom." I found myself grappling with the delicate balancing act that defined contemporary motherhood, that most millennial mothers face. There was a spotlight on the tussle between devotion and vocation.

Juggling being a new mom, wife, and daughter with two jobs, my health was becoming an overwhelming concern. I pinpointed that this was not what I truly wanted in life. I wanted to be able to balance work and fulfilling life to the fullest while also being a great mother. Due to this incredible juggling act, I also started to feel financial stress because I was working TWO jobs, with TWO degrees, and still wasn't fulfilled. Mind you, I also had an incredibly supportive husband and family, but the pressures of society become overwhelming for a 9-5 working mother. This journey I was on really became a pivotal point in my life and directed me to finding a better work-life balance.

So, why did I start my blog for moms? Starting a blog or any business can inspire women to pursue their passion while also getting to be just moms - present moms. This allows mothers flexibility and to prioritize their families while pursuing their work objectives. I wanted to take advantage of the opportunity that my mother didn't have. I want to help other women in the same situation not only raise their children but also pursue their own dreams! I believe that every child deserves to have a loving and dedicated parent, and no one should have to choose between their career and family. With the support of loved ones and a determination to prioritize what truly matters, it's possible to create a life that feels more authentic and satisfying.

My journey first began by realizing that I was just not great at finances - something that was never talked about or taught in my family. My ama had shown me the journal in which she wrote the monthly bills, but that was the extent of money conversations. So as I began my journey as a first-generation professional, I quickly realized how much I avoided money and was uncomfortable with the topic. This sent me on a mission to find someone I could trust, learn, and grow from, and ran into a fellow Latina boss lady who was teaching women of color about finances - my very own financial coach!

Financial coaches are an amazing investment and asset to include in your life, and mine taught me to realize the negative perspective and view I had around money. CRAZY! I learned the various blocks I had which in turn meant that I had some work to do. This is what also ties into my blog!

In my blog Little Liz Things, I share more about how my mentorship process has made a big difference in alleviating many of the financial traumas that were roadblocks to my personal growth and were deterring me from taking the leap into starting my own blogging business to continuously inspire other mothers.

In life, we are all on our own unique journeys shaped by our past and motivated by our dreams. My journey, rooted in my mother's love and inspired by my own experiences, has led me to this point where I'm committed to helping other mothers find the balance, financial literacy, and support they need to thrive!

*Tips and wisdom for other women:*

1. **Foster your community of peers:** Building a support network is essential for personal and professional growth. Surround yourself with individuals who can offer guidance, mentorship, or expertise in areas where you need assistance. Whether it's seeking advice from experienced professionals, connecting with mentors, or collaborating with like-minded peers, your village can provide valuable insights and encouragement to propel you forward. Don't be afraid to ask for help and leverage the collective wisdom of your community.

2. **Build a healthy relationship with money:** Financial literacy is a critical skill that empowers you to make informed decisions about your finances. Take the time to educate yourself about budgeting, investing, saving, and managing debt. If you haven't prioritized financial education in the past, now is an excellent opportunity to start. Whether it's reading books, attending financial workshops, or consulting with a financial advisor, taking control of your financial future is a powerful step toward achieving your goals. Understand that money is a tool that can help you realize your dreams when managed wisely.

3. **Prioritize fun and fulfillment:** Life is a journey, and it's important to savor the moments along the way. Make a conscious effort to prioritize joy and fulfillment in your life. Identify activities, hobbies, and experiences that bring you genuine happiness and align with your passions. These moments of joy not only nourish your soul but also re-energize you for your pursuits. Don't let the pressures of life stifle your sparkle; instead, seek out and embrace the things that make your heart sing. Remember that a balanced life includes moments of happiness and fulfillment, so make time for them.

4. **Embrace Your Passions:** One of the most profound ways to find fulfillment and create a life that truly resonates with your inner self is to wholeheartedly embrace your passions. Often, societal norms and external pressures can steer us away from what we genuinely love and aspire to do. However, by unapologetically embracing your passions, you have the power to carve a unique path that aligns with your values, desires, and dreams.

—Little Liz Things

## Jamie Mychelle Faulcon

Founder of Domvio

https://www.facebook.com/DOMVIO2023

I am a 44-year-old single mother of a now teenage daughter as well as a master's prepared Registered Nurse. I have spent most of my years nursing in the home health and hospice arenas. Currently, outside of my current role as a Quality Review Specialist for a national company, a hospice on-call nurse on weekends, and a hospice admission nurse after hours, I am the owner of Juicy Jems (jewelry) and DOMVIO (domestic violence support).

DOMVIO is my newest venture considering my recent experience with my husband. I have been going through an agonizing healing process mentally, emotionally, and physically. I realized there needs to be more and better support systems for those going through domestic violence. We must start by talking about it. Anything not talked about will continue to live. I decided it was time to speak out about this horrific and barbaric abuse we inflict on others.

# NOT ASHAMED

By Jamie Mychelle Faulcon

My life spiraled out of control back in 2018. My father's mother passed away in February. That was the start of this hell I'm currently coming out of. Following my grandmother's passing, my mom decided to retire from working after YEARS of dedication to her employer. We were all so proud of her. She was so excited. Following her retirement, in July 2018, I took her, my cousin, and my daughter to Georgia on vacation. During that visit to Atlanta, the unthinkable kicked off the downward spiral of my sanity.

My seven-year-old, at the time, was a curious but tiny child for her age. Apparently, when you are wearing black and a black woman, people can't see you while sitting behind everyone watching… A couple stood beside my daughter and covered her up. A GROWN MAN pushed his body into her back, in an attempt to SNATCH MY BABY!! I was watching it all and went BALLISTIC!!! She was saved due to her mom being a COMPLETE, PSYCHOTIC INDIVIDUAL when her daughter was on the line.

Fast forward to August 23, 2018. I walked into my parents' house and my dad stopped me at the door and made me hug him to get in the house. LOL. He loved us so much. My baby BEGGED to stay the night with my parents, so I let her, as usual. I went home, five minutes away from them, and once I got in the house, my mom called me, frantic. She was yelling at my dad. I thought they were arguing, but I didn't hear him in the background. She kept yelling his name. I yelled, "I'm on the way!" I immediately called my oldest sister, Kim, to get her to call my other, sick sister Tina. I lived 3 minutes from Tina. By the time I was passing her house, she was in the car and riding behind me to get to our parents' house. We got Daddy in the car off to the ER. I dropped the kids off with my niece and went straight to the hospital.

When I arrived in the ER, the doctor was in the process of giving my dad TPA for another stroke. While they were preparing the medication, he looked at me and started making faces. He was trying to tell me what was wrong. Anyone who knows me knows I was in a car accident when I was nineteen. Due to hospital NEGLIGENCE, I had a subdural hematoma that was NOT treated. I now have brain damage from that; a meningioma has formed that is inoperable, and I have been diagnosed with migraines and EPILEPSY (aka seizures). I noticed, while he was making faces that he was seizing. I jumped up in NURSE MODE and started to push him on his side. My mom and the nurse started pushing him back towards me. I yelled at them, "HE'S HAVING A SEIZURE!!!" They immediately turned him over, secretions ran out his mouth, and then the doctor decided to hold off on the TPA and do an MRI that showed he had been seizing the entire time.

Within 30 minutes, he had FIVE SEIZURES. On September 7, 2018, he was officially diagnosed with GBM, glioblastoma. GBM-4 is an aggressive brain cancer that is not curable with a life expectancy of 12-18 months. After two brain surgeries, he beat the odds. The only problem was, we lost his nephew, who was like a son to him on March 3, 2019. About two weeks later, my mom's close cousin passed away unexpectedly. Mama was broken.

The next hit came when Mama wasn't feeling well. I took her to the ER. She walked in and nine days later, we had the ambulance take her home on hospice. She was diagnosed with stomach cancer that metastasized to the liver (5 masses), left lung, and spine. She also had a blood clot, 3 blood transfusions, and a filter placed. On March 29, 2019, she came home. March 30, 2019 at 9:14 pm, she took her last breath. She was my best friend; I've been destroyed ever since.

My dad was done. His tumor was gone and nothing was preventing him from living an amazing life. Nothing, except his wife just died. On

June 3, 2019, he told me he was done and wanted to "go home like I took my mama." Those were his words. We did hospice again. Here's the kicker. I'm a hospice RN CASE MANAGER and had been for about ten years prior to them needing hospice, so I was their nurse. My dad died in my arms on July 13, 2019, at 5:42 pm. I was suicidal, and made an attempt. My eight-year-old and paparazzi jewelry saved my life that night.

In October 2020, I met my Mauries. I fell for him hard! He was THE ONE!! There was nothing special about him, but he treated me so well. He was always there for me. We lived together, he asked me to marry him, and I was happy. He was jealous and didn't want me to model, so I backed out. I mostly backed out due to having gastric bypass surgery and I wanted to get my body right. Body dysmorphia IS REAL!

July 30, 2022, we got married! I was so happy. That night, things changed. All of a sudden I became all kinds of nasty. I'm a strong-willed person, so I'm not taking that sitting down; I'm going toe to toe. On September 29th, 2022, we were arguing. He SNAPPED! He choked me and slammed me against the wall. He then slammed me on the bed and was on top of me. I remember thinking, "I'm going to die." My daughter was in the next room. I couldn't get any air in or out. As of today, my vocal cords are still damaged. My voice is rough and manly compared to how soft it had been before. He let go and the police were called. He went to jail for three weeks.

Everyone was telling me he was sick and needed help, so I came up with stipulations and the prosecutor agreed with them. There was counseling and medication. He did everything. I noticed he had the doctor change his medication. I didn't agree with the change, but he didn't want to hear that and did it anyway. Then, I noticed he wasn't taking it. He was putting it in the trash, but was smoking marijuana all day, every day. I worked two jobs to cover the household costs while he did not work. He received a disability benefit of less than

$1000/month. That didn't cover the household bills, much less the rent. Basically, I was the tree, wood, table, plates, food, and the dishwasher while all he brought was his behind to sit and eat.

On March 19, 2023, he totaled my 2020 Dodge Ram Sport Big Horn limited edition with a Hemi pickup truck that was jacked up on spiked 37 in rims. I told him NOT to get in the truck and go anywhere, but low and behold, he took off, no matter what I said, ran a stop sign, caused a MAJOR accident, and now I drive a Ford Escape. I was LIVID!

March 30, 2023, on the fourth anniversary of my mom's death, the UNTHINKABLE happened. I was working and thinking about my mom. I knew I should've taken that day off, but I was going to try to tough it through this year. He slept in. I worked and cried all morning while he slept. He got up and went downstairs. I sat at my desk working. Eventually, I got up around 1:30 pm, put some clothes on and went out. I asked him calmly, "Why do you want to be with me?" It set him off! He started calling me a bitch and whore and telling me I was nasty, etc. I didn't respond. I was tired. I was over it and I was done. He asked if I was going somewhere. I said, "Yes I am. I'd prefer to go alone and will be back soon." He always went with me when I left the house. Today, I needed time to reflect and talk to my mom. He jumped in the rental, told me he was going to make me wreck the rental into the house I was renting, and proceeded to try. I finally got him to stop. I backed up, turned around, and was driving up the path to the main road. I had my seatbelt on. He proceeded to say, "This is what everybody wants anyway." I was confused and before I could say anything, he jumped up, grabbed my head, and started PUNCHING me in the face and head. I broke away, opened the door, and leaned out. I realized my seatbelt was still on and the truck was still in drive. He grabbed my head, pulled me down over the center console, and started punching me in my left temple. I kept screaming for him to

Women Who Lead | 87

stop. I finally put the truck in park and hit the button to take my seatbelt off. He stopped, got out of the truck, slammed the door, and walked off of the driveway and down the street away from the house.

Following the attack, I called 911 and drove directly to the police station. The operator told me to stay on the phone until I arrived. When I pulled up, the officers came and took pictures. I was hysterical. They called an ambulance to take me to get checked out at our local urgent care. My left index finger and middle finger felt broken. My niece had to come pick my daughter up from school. After I finished getting checked out, I had to get an officer to put me in the back of his squad car (I'M CLAUSTROPHOBIC!) to drive me back to the rental truck that he damaged the rearview mirror in, so that I could pick up my baby.

My face was swollen. I had knots on the sides of my face. My left eye remained swollen and I couldn't make a complete fist with my left hand FIVE MONTHS AFTER THE FACT. He busted my right cheek open on the inside to the point that my entire cheek was hanging in my mouth. I couldn't eat for three weeks. My hands had so many cuts, I couldn't grip anything. Again, my 12-year-old had to take care of me. He cut me across my left eye. I have been having migraines since this happened.

He called that night. I answered. He asked if I was home; I said yes. His response was, " I thought they said you had a seizure." His goal was to kill me. He told me on three different occasions he wanted me dead. The medication didn't do it. The counseling didn't stop him. He keeps telling me he's going to get out soon. He was sentenced on July 24, 2023. He received 2 years, 11 months and then he's free from jail. My sentence was LIFE. I now have additional damage to my brain that I have to medicate for. I'm traumatized and trust NO ONE. I can't open my eyes some days and the pain is too much. Emotionally and mentally, I've been on a rollercoaster ride of grief. One day I'm okay, the next I'm angry. The day after that, I miss him. I'm tired of hearing how much he loves me and how he's going to be coming "home" soon. I don't think he will ever understand the trauma he put me through, even though his ex-girlfriend tried to kill him four years ago with a knife. I don't think he cares what he puts us through either.

I know my healing has taken me a while. I don't want to be without him, but I don't want him near me ever again either. His mom has NOT ONCE reached out to me to see if we are okay. The only person in his family that has is Altisha Edmonds, his sister. We don't exist to everyone else. I guess that explains why he's so messed up in the head to the point where he can think he can get away with what he did to me. I'm NOT ASHAMED to tell my story. I'm NOT ASHAMED to start my support business for other ABUSED people, male or female (DOMVIO). I'm NOT ASHAMED to have my family know how I feel and what I've gone through. At the end of the day, this is MY TEST AND MY TESTIMONY and I PRAY it helps the next woman going through what I just came from, all because I'm NOT ASHAMED.

## Diana Svensson

Founder of European Trading Agency

http://linkedin.com/in/dianasvensson
https://www.facebook.com/NordicEntrepreneur
https://instagram.com/nordicentrepreneur
www.dianasvensson.com

I've always been a curious-minded person.

This has led me to become the go-to person when it comes to entrepreneurship, branding, storytelling, marketing, and personal growth.

After earning my marketing degrees, winning multiple awards and scholarships, and becoming a well-known public speaker and a nominee for Female Entrepreneur of the Year 2020, I want nothing else than for people to see who I really am. To see what brought me to where I am and what keeps my torch burning. Because life hasn't been easy in the modern world, and it's safe to say it's time to tell my story and unfold the truth. Now, it's my turn to pass on my knowledge and inspire women around the globe just like you, by sharing my experiences from the eyes of a nervous little girl who left everything she knew to become the strong, bold, and fearless woman she is today.

# THE GREY UNICORN

By Diana Svensson

"Diana! Get a grip. You actually don't think that you can start your own brand, do you?"

"No. You are absolutely right. I will not ONLY start my own brand, but I will become it!"

I hate being challenged. There, I said it.

Even as a little girl, I would be rebellious to the T. It wouldn't matter if it would hurt me or if I'd break an arm trying, but I would never tolerate being told "You can't". Those particular words made my blood boil like no other. But I will be honest and say that changed somewhere along the way…

Growing up in a household where I had to be a parent to my parents and where I cleaned up blood from our wooden floors more often than I played with dolls, my traumatic childhood made me want to escape my reality more than you can imagine. I quickly discovered that one way to do so was to write and that writing was a way to get my feelings and thoughts out of me without having to trust anyone. I could simply write down my thoughts, insecurities, and sometimes even anger, and they would just fade away inside me like they did on the post-it notes I always had in my room.

Little did I know that one day I would get paid to write down other people's thoughts and stories and call myself a copywriter.

One of my clients once asked me, "How do I know what I'm good at? How do I know what I can sell and what service I can provide people? I feel so lost, but I really want to become an entrepreneur!" I asked her a simple question that changed her entire perspective: what do people often ask as a favor from you? What do you actually help people with? THAT is what you should get paid for! Because they call you and ask for your expertise for a reason. You have *something* in you that they need. Now go out there and get *paid* for that something!

The hug she gave me was priceless. But her six-figure recruitment company isn't; in fact, it's worth millions now. And if she can do it, so can you.

Where you end up is not as important as where you start. Not many women are brave enough to take the leap like you and me, and I know you might think "But I don't run a business (yet?)"; but honey, you have already started your journey. You are reading this for a reason.

As I mentioned earlier, life hasn't always been easy for me. I have dealt with many challenges that shaped me into who I am today, and I'll tell you about some of them later on. Furthermore, I named my chapter "The Grey Unicorn" because it describes how I've always felt as a person. Growing up in many different countries and being born and partially raised in Sweden really made me feel connected to the German word "Fernweh" – which means a yearning for distant places and missing places you've never been. Because that's how I feel. I never felt like I belonged somewhere, and I always longed for different places but never felt at home. It's a fascinating feeling that hurts despite it driving me forward, and I know you might have felt that too. Sweden is a great and safe country, but the mentality and culture are somewhat too introverted and calm for my colorful and bold personality. I am always "too much" no matter what I do. So now I have learned to embrace it. I don't think of myself as "too much" or too loud, I just accept that others might be too little.

I realized I was made to become an entrepreneur when I went for a job interview at a shoe store when I was twenty years old. I wore my fanciest suit, had my heels on, and had my hair up in a sleek bun with hoops in my ears. The manager was a tall guy who sat down in front of me and took off his glasses. He looked at me and just asked, "What are you doing here?" I said I was there for the interview and didn't understand why he would ask that. He pointed at the door and said, "I know someone special when I see them. You are not made to be working in my shoe store, but I can definitely see you as a designer for them. Now walk through those doors and come back when you have your business ready because I want to work with you, not above you."

Shocked as I was, I went back home and sat down in front of my computer. I started Googling how to start a business, and some local workshops and events popped up, so I stopped by and the rest is history. But it was just the beginning.

Lesson number one: If someone believes in you, it often means they see something in you that you usually don't.

My mother (who was a florist and whom this chapter is dedicated to) always told me: "Always treat yourself like a flower. Water yourself with energy, positivity, and motivation, and make sure to blossom during the right season. That's when your most colorful self will come out, and that is when people will want you."

She wasn't wrong. I really try to live by those words, and when I started looking at the people around me, I saw energy thieves and friends without ambitions. I never once heard anyone in my surroundings say that they wanted to run a business or take the leap. All I could hear was how secure it was to have a stable 9-5 job along with how comfortable they were. Don't get me wrong, I'm all up for comfort. But I would rather say I lived an exciting and thrilling life than a comfortable one. Just like I would pick boss-babe high heels over any comfortable shoe. Have you ever looked at anyone's shoes and said, "OMG they look so comfy!" Or would you rather have people saying, "OMG where did you get those?"

Lesson number 2: Step out of your comfort zone. Because it's the wall you built around yourself through society's expectations of you, honey.

I grew up with parents who couldn't get along and I have no siblings to turn to. My friends became my siblings, and I trusted them with all I had. You can probably imagine how that turned out.

But I later learned that if you have only ONE person to turn to, you are luckier than many other people on this Earth. Trust and kindness have become so rare that people often mistake them for flirting. But I do have a few people who've been there along the way. The few who rode the Ford with me when the limousine broke down. The few chosen ones who've proven to be the true souls I needed to get through my obstacles and the crazy hard times. They have proven that blood is not always thicker than water and that you're not always stronger alone. So, if you have a huge network now and you (just like I did) have thousands of contacts in your contact list, prepare yourself to lose 90% of them. Yup. You heard me. Once you surround yourself with people who have the same goals, ambitions, and motivations as you, that's when the real success starts. But it is also when the truth hits because I found out this huge lesson the hard way. Are you ready?

Lesson number 3: Not all your friends want to see you succeed.

It's true, I promise. Once I gave birth to my daughter and started my media and communication business back in 2016, it was impossible to get likes from my so-called friends, but I received hundreds of messages from random people who thanked me for my public speaking sessions or for helping my clients to gain their confidence back! I am sure you want to know where I found my own confidence again after being turned down for all the job interviews I went to.

Well, remember how I told you to surround yourself with people who have the same goals, motivations, and ambitions as you? I found them along the way, and they helped me bring back my rebellious side. So, I turned all the "Nos" into "Cans". So, say it out loud with me in a real Eddie Murphy (as Sherman Klump) kind of voice.

Lesson number 4:YES. I. CAN!

As we are approaching the final lines in my chapter, I want to pass on some more advice to you so you don't have to make the same mistakes that I did when I just started my entrepreneurial journey. I want you to take notes and really let my words sink in because I'm sharing things with you that I wish I had known as a rookie. Jokes aside.

- Laugh. If sh*t hits the fan, just laugh. Life is too short to stop laughing and it will make you feel better for a few seconds. Those are seconds you could've spent mad as hell that you'll never be able to get back.

- I said it before, and I'll say it again: Surround yourself with people you want to be like. Aspiring, strong, and bold women who don't obey society's norms.

- Dare to become who you want to be. Otherwise, you wouldn't be reading this. You would watch a miserable show on NETFLIX and dwell on your life.

- This might hit a personal spot in you, but you don't have to become like your parents. You are not them. Neither do you need to have their expectations put upon yourself.

- It's OK to cry, just remember that the feeling will pass.

- Have ALL your agreements with people written down. Whether it's in an email, on a post-it, or in a word-doc. Just write it down. And make sure the other person keeps a signed copy. This would've saved me so much headache, speaking of crying.

- HAVE FUN! If you're not having fun, it's not going to work out. Passion for your product or service must come from YOU. If you are not passionate about what you bring to the table – why should your consumers be?

And I'll leave you with my mother's words again:

> "Always treat yourself like a flower. Water yourself with energy, positivity, and motivation, and make sure to blossom during the right season. That's when your most colorful self will come out, and that is when people will want you."

*1960 – 2021*
*In loving memory of Hengameh Sattarzadeh*

## Grainne Fletcher

Founder of Team Hearts ANZ

https://www.facebook.com/grainnethecoach
https://www.instagram.com/grainne_fletcher
www.ladycollagen.lifevantage.com

Grainne is originally from Ireland and has an adventurous spirit, sailing around the world in her 20s before residing in Australia. Grainne then went on to have a 20-year career owning traditional businesses before transitioning into the health and wellness industry nine years ago.

In that time, Grainne and her team have grown a multi-million dollar business that has expanded across the globe to the USA, Europe, Asia, Australia, and New Zealand. She is passionate about people learning how to stay healthier for longer and knows the secrets to youthful aging using natural products.

Grainne loves to teach people about residual income and how they can create a legacy business that enables people to work from home, or anywhere in the world. Her team is made up of stay-at-home mums, teachers, and CEOs looking for a flexible lifestyle and an extra stream of income.

Grainne resides in Australia with her two children, Harry and Ruby, her husband Darren, and two dogs.

# WIIFT (WHAT'S IN IT FOR THEM) IT'S WHAT I LIVE BY.

By Grainne Fletcher

Growing up in Ireland my family delighted in recounting how I was definitely not shy and the talker of the family. I loved to connect with people of all ages and would ask lots of questions. I was genuinely interested in knowing everything about them, and I believe this intrinsic trait has been a gift that allowed me to forge connections and excel beyond measure in life.

Beginning a new chapter at the age of 22, I left Ireland behind and embraced the vast landscapes of Australia. My years combined travel and exploration, each experience enriching my perspective. Amidst the journey, destiny transformed my path. There is a saying that there are two pivotal opportunities in your life — one before the age of forty, and the other after. It was during this time that a girlfriend shared a proposition and so I embarked on a new venture—starting a recruitment agency. My partner and I navigated the industry with remarkable success over eight fruitful years, ending in the agency's eventual sale, a testament to the power of curiosity and seizing the right opportunity.

I spent the next several years helping my husband establish his clinic, which was great, but I did start to wonder if there was more to life. His job was very fulfilling but I didn't feel I was living my purpose. I worked long hours and during school holidays, felt the "mum guilt", and thought there had to be more to life. Remember, I said another opportunity would come along after your 40s; well it did and I was open to taking a look.

Network marketing came into my life by chance when I took some weight loss products. I saw someone present about the topic and I thought, "If he can do it why can't I?" There is nothing special about the person upfront; they just pushed back fear and took a risk.

I was coachable and teachable and learned fast. My motto was not "fake it till you make it", but "faith it till you make it." Sometimes you have to take a chance in life you know deep down inside is your purpose, and you have to push fear out of the way and take a risk.

I decided to live by 2 acronyms and it has helped me grow in my career. FEAR is not something to be afraid of, whether fear of public speaking or fear of man. I decided to change my mindset and say FEAR is feeling excited and ready. Taking risks in life is what we all have to take some time to get ahead. For me, RISK is Relationships, Integrity, Service, and Kindness. If I develop good relationships with my team and customers I will succeed. I have integrity in everything I do and give incredible service. Last but not least is to have kindness with everyone. I love the saying it's nice to be important but it's more important to be nice.

Seven years ago I went looking for my forever home in another company. I wanted a company that was backed by science, where products were catalysts for transformative change in people's lives; a cause I could wholeheartedly champion. The products they offered had to be accessible and authentic, unique, pure, and affordable. The products I found are activators and not supplements so they switch on pathways in your body so that your body is working at its optimum.

Then I had to find the right leader, which is so important to align yourself with. As I am a Christian, I wanted to align myself with someone with the same values. I wanted the teachings and message not to be about flash cars and yachts and vision boards but about what we could do for other people and the impact we could have in the world.

I prayed and started Googling and found the perfect person. I emailed her and basically said, "We are 6 women in Australia who are

Christians and we believe that LifeVantage is the company that we are meant to launch in Australia. Could we launch your team here?"

They say that when you find a job you love you will never work another day in your life. Well, that is me; I found a product that slows down aging by turning on your body's abilities to make its own antioxidants. In 7 years, my team and I have helped thousands of customers get their lives back on track, and I get to hear incredible, life-changing stories every day. I get the honor of changing people's lives every day.

We launched in Australia in 2016. "Faith it till you make it" is exactly what we did. I truly knew that God had given me this opportunity. We were so passionate about these products and the lives we were going to change. We left FEAR at the door and took the biggest RISK of our lives and it paid off. I quickly advanced to being a top leader in Australia and then had the opportunity to open the company in New Zealand. I spent a year working with the company with 6 other leaders to make it the most successful country launch the company ever had.

I have never been a person who wants to climb to the top without everyone else. I want to see people succeed and I live by Zig Ziglar's quote: "You can have everything you want, if you help enough people get what they want."

One of the greatest skills you can learn is how to understand people. Ask great questions and learn to be quiet. God gave us two ears and one mouth for a reason, and I have learned to be a great listener. By asking lots of questions you can work out what type of person you are speaking to. A great little exercise I do once I meet a person is to work out what type of personality they have. This can literally take two minutes.

I go by Dani Johnson's gem personalities.

RUBY is a very driven person, "Give me the trailer, not the movie", no stories just the end goal, and they ask "Will it work for me?"

SAPPHIRE loves being around people, is a fun person, and is always happy and high-energy.

PEARL loves to really help people, is the first one there to make the dinner look out for people, and genuinely cares about people.

EMERALD is a very analytical, research-focused, and extremely organized person.

I know how to talk to people about my products or about business opportunities by working out what personality they are.

WIIFT ( what's in it for them ) is what I live by asking great questions in all aspects of my life so I can work out what others would like to hear and give them the information they want.

I changed my mindset on finances as well. I became very careful with my language and what words I would use about myself and about my financial situation. What you think about, you bring about. Money in the right hands can change the world. I have always tithed and given to charities, and I understand the laws of money.

I love to help people dream again and think differently. We have been conditioned to work 40 hours a week for 40 years, and most people don't live with purpose. They are just surviving. I believe every family should have a side hustle or an online business that brings in residual income into the home. Residual income is money that keeps coming in even though the work has stopped. You never know when life throws a curveball at you and one day you may not be able to work.

Two years ago I had family issues and basically needed to walk away from my business for over a year. In that time I kept getting paid the exact same money as before because of residual income. My customers stayed on products, my team kept their businesses going, and I could be with my family which is where I needed to be.

If you want to be at home with your kids, or head off traveling the world, the business goes with you and enables you to live the life of your dreams. This is a legacy business that can be willed to your children, so you can make a difference in your family's life for generations to come.

You may decide to volunteer overseas, which is what I want to do when my kids leave home and travel the world with my husband. You can do these things as well if you don't let fear hold you back and you take that risk in life. You get one chance in life to make a difference and feel fulfilled, and I thank God every day for the life he has given me. I want to do his will on Earth and treat people with love and kindness, which in the end will give me true happiness.

## Londell J Cox

CEO of Divine Retreats & Tours, LLC

https://www.linkedin.com/in/londellcox
https://www.facebook.com/panworld123
https://www.instagram.com/divineretreatstours
https://divinetravelpal.com
https://www.divineretreatstours.com

Londell J. Cox is the Founder/CEO of Divine Retreats & Tours, LLC.

Londell has been involved in multiple start-ups, and no matter where she worked, she always seemed to return to her first love…entrepreneurship; entrepreneurship seems to be in her DNA.

Londell graduated Magna Cum Laude with a Bachelor of Arts Degree in Psychology and later acquired a Master's Degree in Business Administration with a concentration in Marketing Management.

Londell hails from the beautiful island of Trinidad & Tobago, and although she's lived some thirty-plus years in New York City, she still has the heart of an island girl.

The sky is the limit for Londell, and on any given day she can be found serving her clients at her home office in New York City. Londell's company specializes in group/faith-based travel.

When asked what keeps her going, Londell replied, "My faith, God is the center of my universe."

# ANOTHER BUSINESS AGAIN?

By Londell J Cox

Divine Retreats & Tours, LLC; that was the name of my new business. I launched my travel company on January 5$^{th}$, 2018. It was the culmination of all the knowledge I had acquired from my academic career and the expertise I had garnered from managing my previous businesses. However, I could not have been prepared for COVID-19, in fact, I was planning to host a group of clients to visit the steps of the Apostle Paul in Greece and Turkey, and it was supposed to be my first international tour. I was really looking forward to this trip, especially since so far I had only done bus tours within the United States. At the onset, my business plan included domestic and international tours with group faith-based tours being my primary niche. Unlike my other businesses, I was sticking with this one no matter what, simply because I had made a promise to God that come what may I was not going to ditch this business. I was going to press on when the going got tough, but by no means did I expect a deadly pandemic.

Despite the pandemic I still managed to keep my virtual doors open - it is one of the great benefits of having a fully operational online travel business. One might be inclined to say that in today's world it is easier to just book your own travel online, but travel professionals are necessary. Luxury travel, group travel, destination weddings, and more complex travel involving multiple cities are just a few of the areas where travel consultants really excel. In addition, at Divine, we are also able to book private yachts, jets, helicopters, limos, assist with passport renewals, visas, Super Bowl tickets, US Open tickets, and book really off-the-grid exotic destinations. There is a misconception that using a travel advisor is more expensive. I beg to differ. The only way that can occur is if the agent charges you a fee for his/her research, and in that case, they will inform you upfront. In fact, using an advisor is safer because things can and do sometimes go wrong when on vacation, and it is comforting to have a travel professional to assist you in navigating the situation.

How did I get here? I was born Londell J. Phillips on the beautiful twin island nation of Trinidad and Tobago. I was not raised by my biological parents, but in the Caribbean it was common to be raised by grandparents, aunties, and sometimes even good friends. Given the circumstances, my father had made the best decision to leave me in Trinidad with Sylvia while he pursued his ambitions. My dad was an expert at securing great talent; I would later learn firsthand that he knew the most qualified person for every task, whether it was in his business life or his social life. Although Sylvia was not my biological mother, she was the only mother I knew. Sylvia…I can barely say her name without my mind conjuring up sweet memories of my childhood and the woman who raised me with a love that I rarely see today.

Eventually, I would set out for the US to study cosmetology for one year. One year turned to two, two to four and, aside from a short stint back in Trinidad to launch my first business, the damage was done. I left Trinidad in 1987 and let us just say I am one of those people who found themselves at ground zero when the COVID-19 pandemic decimated NYC. The US represented freedom and unlimited possibilities to me, and later while attending college I would read Plato's *Allegory of the Cave* which brought me some comfort because I now understood why I was having difficulty returning home.

Even though entrepreneurship was my first love, I still managed to pursue some of my other aspirations. I believe that people should continue to learn in whichever field they choose. In my mid-twenties I secured a position at an investment bank in Midtown, Manhattan, NYC, and unexpectedly an accident on my way to work would not only take me out of the game but change the trajectory of my life. The days of the golden child were over, and I would learn some of the hardest and most important lessons a human being can learn. While in my quest to get back into corporate America and "the world of work," I was slowly going through my own metamorphosis. Still a newlywed, and unemployed with an eight-month-old, my husband and I made the decision for me to return to school at night, while I raised my daughter Alexia in the daytime. The opportunity to be a stay-at-home mom was one of the greatest blessings to me. Another reason I love entrepreneurship is because it gave me the flexibility to be with my family when they needed me, and I them. Also, even at that time, I still did not know who my biological mother was, and as a result, I was not going to outsource motherhood.

In every gray cloud there is a silver lining. In 2004 I would graduate Magna Cum Laude with a Bachelor's Degree in Psychology, from Medgar Evers College in Brooklyn, and later I graduated from the Florida Institute of Technology with a Master's Degree in Business Administration and a concentration in Marketing Management. Aside from my academic aspirations, over the years I developed a closer relationship with God. I credit Sylvia for teaching me about the Creator early on, and the Emmaus Seventh Day Adventist Church in Brooklyn for reinforcing those early lessons; it would come to pass that my survival depended on it. It seemed like I was constantly playing catchup in a world that I was not familiar with, and living in Brooklyn was vastly different from living in Trinidad. I was always bright-eyed and bushy-tailed when it came to meeting new people and experiencing new cultures, but like any prodigal son I soon longed for my life in Trinidad. What I would have done to know all my neighbors again, or to see kind friendly faces when I walked down the street. I had found myself in a place where God was not an option but a necessity. A mirage is the only way I could describe it…a mirage.

Whenever we meet new people, oftentimes we don't think of the experiences that molded them into who they are. Sometimes you are not responsible for who you become until you have reached that level of consciousness that allows you to recognize that change may be necessary in order to survive, and thrive in whatever organization, church, family, or group you find yourself in. For me it was important that I did not compromise my integrity in my day-to-day interactions with others. Oftentimes not conforming to the status quo can make you very unpopular, but I always knew who I served, and as a result, I have always slept well at night. God created us all the same and different at the same time, and as a Black Caribbean woman living in the US, I quickly learned to embrace all that is me. My mom had raised an independent thinker, which meant anywhere I went that challenged that, there was going to be a problem. I distinctly remember when I was a little girl, four years old to be exact, my mother/Sylvia took me to purchase a pair of dress shoes which I would have worn to church or any formal occasion. My mother told me to choose the color of shoes that I wanted. I chose a red pair that I wore everywhere.

There is a saying that goes, "The way you do one thing is the way you do everything." Ha! I beg to differ; the Bible says, "With God all things are possible." God fills in all the gaps, in business, in school, in ministry, and all the areas of life where you might be inadequate. I can testify to that. It's the reason why it was so important that my life be in alignment with God. "Try driving a car that needs alignment and see how far it will take you." My journey involved aligning: my family life, my business/career, and my faith, which is no easy task by any stretch of the imagination, but possible. My business experience, my academic prowess, and my faith are the perfect combination for my success.

## Prudence Hatchett

PH Counseling, LLC
Mental Wellness Specialist

www.linkedin.com/in/prudencehatchett
https://www.facebook.com/phcounselingllc
https://www.phcounseling.org/
https://learn-with-prudence.myshopify.com/

Prudence Hatchett earned a B.A. in Psychology and a M.S. in Special Education with a concentration in Emotional Disability (Mississippi State University). She earned an M.Ed. in Counselor Education and completed the Master's Emotional Disability Endorsement Program in Education (University of Mississippi). She is a nationally certified Counselor, Licensed Professional Counselor (LPC), Board Qualified Supervisor, Board Certified Telemental Health Provider, Certified Clinical Anxiety Treatment Professional, Certified Grief Professional, Advanced Certified Autism Specialist, Certified Addictions-Informed Mental Health Professional, Certified Employee Assistance Professional, US DOT Substance Abuse Professional, and a Board Certified Coach. She holds a Master's level educator's license with educational endorsements in the areas of Guidance Counseling, Mild/Moderate Disabilities, Emotional Disability, and Psychology.

Prudence opened her private practice, PH Counseling, LLC, in 2018 and offers a variety of services. In 2023, she was named a Subject Matter Expert for the National Board of Certified Counselors, Inc. and Affiliates.

# THE POWER SOURCE:
# HOW I FOUND FREEDOM FROM IMPOSTER SYNDROME
# BY LEARNING TO TRUST MYSELF

By Prudence Hatchett

Resilient. Authoritative. Assertive. Confident. Empowered. These are the words that come to mind if someone asked me to describe myself today. Shy. Bashful. Unsure. Confused. Stiff. These are the words that would come to mind if someone had asked me to describe myself 15 years ago. There is a big difference between the two sets of descriptions. It took me a long time to gain the confidence described in the first set of words. And no, it wasn't just wishful thinking or pure luck. It was dedication, consistency, and preparation. I had to learn how to manage and bounce back from disappointments, failure, negativity, and the dreaded beast that is called imposter syndrome.

I'm currently in my 40s, 41 years old to be exact, and my life has never been better.

And guess what? I'm going to shake my magical wand, unleash my manifestation power and state, "I expect my life to continue to get even better." The best part is I get to choose what "better" actually means for me. It may or may not match someone else's definition and this is ok. Every day, I must choose to walk with my own confidence and authenticity.

Did you notice the word "freedom" is in the title of my chapter? I am choosing to live in the freedom that I have created through education, resiliency, and opportunities. Individual freedom can be mistaken for arrogance if the freedom is presumed to be superficial. I can tell you wholeheartedly that this freedom came from within me, from within my soul, from within my authentic self. What I create through my own freedom, no one else can take away. They don't have the authority to unless I yield that authority to them. Travel back in time with me as I tell you my own story of how I found freedom by learning to trust myself.

Traveling back to 15 years ago, I was quiet and a little shy, not wanting to bring a lot of attention to myself. Maybe I didn't want the attention because people might identify flaws or weaknesses that I wasn't ready to confront. I would ultimately shrink myself to fade into the crowd. I was always socially appropriate, meaning I was respectful, displayed positive social skills, and got along well with others. Although nothing was terribly wrong, I felt like I was out of place. I felt like a stranger in my surroundings. To be honest, I was a stranger in my surroundings because I was not being my authentic self (which I didn't understand until later).

Things started to change when I delved further into my educational career and started to gravitate towards my passions. In my career, I was able to merge my two loves: mental health and education. This is where I started to find my place in the world. Don't get me wrong, this didn't come without hard work, dedication, sleepless nights, and financial strain. The more I learned about mental health and education, the more alive I felt. Feeling alive was equal to being excited to share my knowledge with others instead of fading into the crowd hoping to become invisible. I was operating in my space, or you can say "I was operating in my gifting."

Something was triggered that gave me the power and stability I needed to trust myself. This "power" I am referring to is an unleashing of something that was hidden. Think about a superhero who was put to sleep and buried alive by a wicked witch, but 10 years later someone created a magical potion to pour over the hero as they slept. Then suddenly, the superhero burst out of the ground, flying high to reclaim their rightful position. In turn, this created a very "powerful" scene for the storyline illustrating the hero's comeback victory. Like the superhero, I was becoming more of my authentic self, creating a powerful scene for my own storyline.

As I started to feel better internally, my confidence grew externally. For me, confidence wasn't just about a feeling, it was about action. Hiding myself or shrinking my talents in fear of being called out for having flaws was literally suffocating me. I was fighting against imposter syndrome, and it was exhausting. Because I am in favor of authenticity, it is important for me to note that no one told me to shrink myself. This is something I chose to do based on my own insecurity and self-doubts. I had to learn to counter the imposter syndrome with a new behavior.

I countered the imposter syndrome with confidence. Meaning, I learned to trust my education and skills instead of depending on my feelings. My feelings would change from day to day, and even change directions on the same day. My feelings were not consistent, so I couldn't depend on my feelings to grow my confidence. I had to depend on what I could do because my skills were consistent and steadily growing because I was actively learning. And guess what? I am still actively learning. Remember earlier when I said I expected my life to get even better? That statement wasn't based on a feeling, it was based on my continued willingness to pursue "better" via active learning, which is something I control. Active learning includes reading, researching, planning, and participating in my chosen activities and not passively waiting for someone else to give me the information I need. The more I learned, the more my confidence increased.

Let me back up a bit. This confidence did not occur overnight; there were many steps involved. One step included self-awareness. I had to take a serious look within to help uncover why I was feeling out of place and the barriers blocking my freedom. This also meant that I had to confront my fears of exposing my flaws. The barriers I discovered were mainly mental barriers such as low confidence, anxiety, thought distortions, and hurt feelings. Another barrier included a lack of knowledge or misinformation about what I said I wanted. There is a big difference between "what I want" and "what I am prepared for." The phrase "what I want" is only connected to a feeling, which can't be trusted. Preparation is connected to taking some sort of action, which highlights skill level and strengths. Again, actively learning is what helped provide me with a confidence boost. I can trust what I learn and the facts that I know.

Earlier, I discussed replacing imposter syndrome with a new behavior. When it comes to changing behaviors, identifying a replacement behavior is key. When there is no replacement behavior, old habits take over whether they are good or bad. For example, a person may state, "I want to stop smoking," as a full sentence. However, it should only be a pause. A replacement behavior needs to be identified to help increase the probability of reaching the goal. For example, the statement should be, "I want to stop smoking and improve my quality of breathing so I can walk faster." That way you are intentionally telling the brain what to do. If the brain doesn't know what to do, it will revert to the old habit of smoking, leaving you feeling defeated and exhausted.

For lasting change to take place, I think a positive, strength-based approach is best. A negative approach such as self-criticism can eventually lead to self-punishment, which prolongs improvement. The strength-based approach is a celebration of who you are and who you are becoming. These strengths may include active learning, increased knowledge, hobbies, interests, natural talents, etc. You must recognize and be willing to showcase those strengths. Remember, you can trust and depend on what you can do and act out. In turn, getting rid of the block that is imposter syndrome.

Lastly, this journey is about self-growth and sharing a message of self-healing. When it comes to my career and helping people identify more of who they are, I have a phrase that I like to repeat. It's a direct quote from the front page of my website. The quote is, "Life is a growth experience with all parts working together to mature a healthy and whole individual." Growth is on a continuum, and it never stops. It's almost like we continue to unlock new levels by actively learning more about who we are, gaining insight into the authentic self. I'm finally at a place where I am learning to be more authentic and living out my truths by not pretending to be someone else or fading into the background. Finding freedom from imposter syndrome helped me become more active and resilient. This freedom afforded me the confidence to dream big and pursue my goals. I discovered and activated my own power source by learning to trust myself.

—Prudence Hatchett

## Nicole Villanueva

Savvi Brand Partner
Coach

www.facebook.com/nicole.villanueva.927
https://www.instagram.com/nicole_a_villanueva/
https://www.savvi.com/shopwithmenicolev

Nicole Villanueva is an Ironman, CPT, entrepreneur, and has worked in the healthcare industry for over 15 years. Raised in Secaucus, NJ, she moved to Florida in 2006 and currently lives in Tampa. New challenges excite her and is a firm believer in grabbing every opportunity that comes your way.

She is a Brand Partner with Savvi, a lifestyle company that leads by serving others and aims to provide products that promote confidence and help women feel comfortable in their own skin.

Nicole is a huge dog lover and adopting her pup Cleapatra Mae has brought her so much happiness. She loves to run and enjoys being part of her BLUSH boot camp community, a place that helps women feel stronger mentally and physically. "Just because something is hard, does not mean it is impossible."

# I FINALLY GOT OUT OF MY OWN WAY

By Nicole Villanueva

Remember all those chances you didn't take? What held you back? Was it noise from other people? Was it your mind talking you out of it?

Maybe it's time management, not knowing where to begin, or just being afraid of failure. I am here to tell you to just start! But these are all the things you probably already knew or read before, so why is my story any different?

I didn't always have the most confidence, but walked around without fear if that even makes sense! In high school I was told I would never get into my dream college and that I should have a backup plan. In my mind I was going to be accepted and I was. I had to take summer classes in order to be an official freshman that fall, but early on I learned you never need to change your initial goals, you may just need to change your plan to achieve them.

My stint at my dream school only lasted 2 1/2 years and I unfortunately developed an eating disorder along the way. The pressures of looking good and standing out got the best of me. I can remember fainting at a gym. I don't think I ever told my mother that! I eventually returned to my hometown and was able to keep it somewhat under control. In my 20s my family moved to Massachusetts and I followed them thinking I could have a fresh start. I worked in the hospitality industry for years and was just trying to enjoy being a young adult. I was involved in my first long-term relationship which didn't end the way I hoped. It left me with a lot of emotional baggage, insecurities, and triggered some of my unhealthy body issues.

I can recall lacking self-confidence and being naïve. I was the one that always trusted too easily, the overthinker who cared what others thought of me. I was agreeable to many things at times just for approval. A serial people pleaser. Often smiling on the outside yet crying inside. I was involved in another relationship which was physically abusive, and it stripped me of a lot of my self-respect. For a long time, I relied on alcohol to numb my emotional pain. I was a body shamer and I hated what I saw in the mirror. Even though I was surrounded by a lot of love from family and friends, I often felt alone because I didn't really like myself. I lived that way for many years.

Through therapy I was able to tackle my demons and accept it was a crisis of low self-esteem, but it was something that haunted me from time to time. I kept that story in a box for so many years, but wanted to share it in hopes of helping one person that may relate.

My 30s were a bit of a blur! I choose not to focus on the negative impacts from my previous relationships, but instead on what I learned and how those experiences made me want to work even harder. I knew I was worth so much more but getting myself to believe it was part of my battle.

Fast forward to my 40s. I met some friends at a gym who I instantly connected with. They were training for triathlons, a world I knew nothing about. I thought to myself, "who wakes up at 4:45AM to ride their bike for 7 hours?" I didn't fully understand it but I loved their energy and positive vibes. In 2019, they were participating in an Ironman in Panama City, Florida. Since I was going to support them and cheer them on, I decided to volunteer at the race. To say I was in serious awe of what I saw is an understatement. I left there thinking, *these people are all nuts and I want in.*

The following year they had decided to train for Ironman Cozumel. After some convincing, I took a leap of faith and registered. I had no idea how I was going to accomplish it, but I was finally surrounded by the right people that believed in me when I didn't believe in myself. As of January 2020, I could barely swim laps in a pool or clip in and out of a bike without falling. I continued to get more frustrated and felt uncomfortable trying to swim in open water. I went to a swim clinic to work on my technique. I remember feeling so embarrassed because I could not keep up with the group and felt very out of place.

Was it easy? NO! Did I have a lot of self-doubt and cry often? Of course! Was I hungry all the time? VERY! Did I deal with moments of anxiety at first not knowing if I could pull this off? Absolutely!!!!

But I kept going.

Since every shorter distance race was canceled due to Covid, I had people actually laugh at me and think I was insane to just show up at an Ironman having never done a triathlon in my life. Thinking about it now, I may have been a bit crazy, but I had full support from my family and friends, and as training progressed my confidence was building more and more. At that point I realized, laugh at me and doubt me, I will work even harder and prove you wrong, and I did!!

I was told exactly what I needed to do to accomplish my goal and I listened! I was coachable, and I really wanted to prove to MYSELF I could achieve this! On race day I woke up surprisingly calm. I knew I trained as hard as I could for this moment, and I prayed it would all come together.

It took me 7 minutes and 56 seconds to calm down at the start of the 2.4 mile swim, but once I got my stride I just kept going. I got a flat tire in mile 3 of the 112 mile bike course. I panicked a little, and my confidence was tested, but once I got it changed and pulled myself together, I kept going. During the entire bike course, I had no idea of the actual time because my watch was stuck in run mode. The wind was powerful since there was a storm a few days before, and there was a potential risk of the race being canceled. It was getting later in the day and I knew I was approaching one hell of a final lap on my bike. I can remember cursing and being so angry, but I knew this was going to be my test of mental strength. I was not as worried about my legs giving out but the thoughts in my head I was fighting with. It truly all begins and ends in our minds. By the time I got on my feet to the 26.2 mile run, I knew all those years of self-doubt were just past chapters of my life. I was changing my story. Not all the participants that day finished in time to claim the title, but on Nov, 22, 2020 I did and I became an Ironman. Finishing the race was just an added bonus. The real accomplishment for me was the journey to get there, and I am proud of every mile it took. I will continue to push beyond my boundaries and stay out of my own damn way!

After my Ironman experience, I knew there was no turning back to the person I once was. I conquered my fear of public speaking and gave my personal testimony for a previous company I was with in front of hundreds of people. Although still in healthcare, I left a company of 16 years to start a new career. This December I am blessed to say I will be celebrating my 50th birthday and celebrated myself with a boudoir session this summer. Perfect gift for a recovered body shamer! EVERY woman should do one! Thanks to Jess Veguez Photography.

My mission is to help every woman feel confident and brave. I am PROUD to be partnered with Savvi. A company that was born during the Covid pandemic. We are a top lifestyle brand for ultimate self-care and our goal is to help ALL women feel exceptional in their skin. We have a strong focus on body positivity, inclusivity, and ethnic diversity. We lead with love and win by serving others while helping our community to LOOK good, FEEL good and DO good!

Don't get stuck in the comfort trap. Progress doesn't happen there. Take steps every day to move forward and grab all the opportunities to make an impact. Now more than ever the world needs your special gifts, and PLEASE, stay out of your own way!!!

## Gina Stockdall

Marilyn Jeanne Designs, LLC
Graphic Designer

https://www.linkedin.com/company/marilynjeannedesigns
www.facebook.com/marilynjeannedesigns
www.instagram.com/marilynjeannedesigns
www.marilynjeannedesigns.com

Gina Stockdall has been working in graphic design and marketing since 2021. After graduating with her degree in Multimedia Design and Development, she decided to open her own freelance design business, Marilyn Jeanne Designs, LLC. After partnering with nonprofits like Faith United Methodist Church, Strong Tower Haiti, and 10.18 Strategy, she has grown to offer web, business, print design, social media management and marketing, custom branded merchandise, and marketing consulting. Gina loves making new friends, cooking, baking, playing with makeup, chasing after her two boys, and going on nature walks with her husband.

# THERE'S JUST NOT ENOUGH TIME

By Gina Stockdall

In 2017, I found out I was pregnant with my oldest son. Shortly afterward, I decided I wanted to go back to college (I had previously failed out after leaving an abusive relationship). The job I had at the time made me miserable and I did not want my child to grow up watching me go to a job that drained the life out of me. Fast forward four years (and another baby), and I graduated with my Bachelor's Degree in Multimedia Design and Development from DeVry University. However, by the time I graduated, I had been a stay-at-home mom for two years and COVID had created global shutdowns. I knew I did not want to go back to a traditional office job, but I also wanted to pursue my passions. So, I decided to start my own online business. This way I could pursue a career in design while staying home with my boys.

I started Marilyn Jeanne Designs, LLC in February 2021 with an old laptop in my kitchen. I decided to name the business after my late grandmother who passed away from COVID in May of 2020. I began by dipping my toe into creating custom merchandise and doing freelance graphic design work. However, as time progressed, the business morphed a few times and now we are a marketing and design agency for nonprofits and churches. This type of work can be quite demanding, which gets challenging when you are a wife and mother on top of being a business owner. I found myself overwhelmed and stressed every day when I looked at my daily to-do list. I felt like there just weren't enough hours in the day!

Honestly, the biggest mistake I made as a business owner, wife, and mother was expecting instant success. We live in a society where we expect instant gratification, and that just simply is not realistic. When

I opened my business, for some reason I expected people to just line up around the block (figuratively speaking) for designs and merchandise. Boy, I was in for a rude awakening, wasn't I? I had quite a few custom t-shirt orders come in at first. Then a few logos and business card designs. I was so thankful for anyone who was willing to hire me that I would say "yes" to anyone who asked if I could design or create something. I was running myself ragged. Not to mention I still had to take care of my then 3-year-old and seven-month-old sons, do the household chores, and keep up with my church volunteer duties. I honestly considered closing the business multiple times, but I kept reminding myself that I worked way too hard to just give up. I had to keep pushing forward. However, I needed a better plan of action.

I truly believe a good dose of reality is good for us female entrepreneurs. We are dreamers. We are go-getters. We explore paths and avenues that no one else has ever dared to go down. However, we have to do these things with reality and our families in mind. As a woman who wants to lead, you can do anything that you set your mind to. You just have to use realistic and attainable steps to get there. You also have to remember that you started this business so you could have freedom. Do not let yourself be so addicted to chasing your next big payday that you forget to create a life with your family and loved ones. Because ultimately, they are the reason behind all of your hard work, aren't they? You work long, exhausting hours so you can provide for your family, to give them a better life than you had. But something I want you to remember is that your time with your loved ones is limited. Do not think that you can spend more time with them tomorrow because tomorrow is never promised to any of us. So, how do we find our proper work-life balance?

The key to a practical work-life balance is creating a schedule that gives you your dream life. Here is an example of my daily routine: I wake up at four o'clock in the morning to feed my cat, read my daily Bible reading, and then get in a thirty-minute workout. After that, I make breakfast for the family, get myself and the boys ready for the day, start a load of laundry, make a cup of coffee, and take the boys outside in the yard or on a local hiking trail. At nine o'clock, the boys and I start our daily chores. We will do this together until eleven-thirty. They eat lunch while I finish cleaning up the kitchen. After lunch, the boys take an afternoon nap and I start my afternoon office hours. I will wrap up my afternoon office hours around four and then we do a family walk (or board game if it is raining or too cold/hot). Dinner preparation starts promptly at five, we eat at five-thirty, and spend time together as a family until six-thirty. My evening office hours are from six-thirty to nine while my husband spends one-on-one time with the kids. I know it sounds like a lot, but honestly, this is the life I have always dreamed of. I get to stay home and enjoy my children, I stay on top of the house while teaching my boys responsibility, we consciously make time during our busy schedules to spend time together as a family, and I get to grow my business. It is hard some days, but I would not trade it for anything.

So, how did I create a schedule that helps me grow my business at a realistic rate while tending to my young children and home? The first step is writing down your non-negotiables. My personal non-negotiables are that I will spend mornings with my children and take care of our home. It is easier for me to focus on my business when I know my family is already taken care of. I will not work on birthdays, holidays, or any day that has a special event (graduations, school parties, etc.). I also will eat dinner with my family at the table each and every day. Whatever is close to your heart, write it down.

After you have your non-negotiable list, figure out what time of day those special times occur and block them out on your calendar. Do not give your clients the option to even book a meeting during those times. Creating clear and hard boundaries is going to keep you from getting overwhelmed, help you not be walked on like a doormat, and create a respectful work relationship between you and your client.

Step three is to set your office hours. The best way to do this is to figure out when you are the most productive. For myself, I am the most productive in the afternoons and evenings, hence why my office hours are noon to four and then six-thirty to nine. Plus, doing a time block schedule like this actually helps you be more productive in the long run because you cannot waste time doing tasks that won't propel your business forward because your work time is limited. Another thing to always remember is that being busy does not always equate to being productive. So make sure that your to-do list only has productive tasks each day.

Step four is to write down a list of things that bring you joy. For example, I love to cook and bake. It brings me such peace and joy to make things for my family. So, now I have a designated day each week where I make an entire meal and dessert from scratch for them, and we all look forward to it. I even have my boys help me in the kitchen for extra bonding time. Once you know what brings you joy, go back to your calendar and sprinkle in some time each week to do those things. This is how you achieve a beautiful work-life balance. You are able to never miss another important family event, you are doing things that spark your joy, and you are being purposeful in becoming the professional that you intend to be. It took me a while to get here, but I will never be going back to the lies of hustle culture again. I worked hard to create this beautiful life, and you can too. I believe in you.

## Samantha Bearman

Founder of Bear Cave Productions, LLC

https://www.linkedin.com/in/samanthabearman/
https://www.facebook.com/p/Bear-Cave-Comedy-100089878433205/
www.instagram.com/sambearcomedy
www.samanthabearman.com
www.bearcavecomedy.com

Samantha Bearman, known as Sam Bear, originates from Santa Barbara, CA. She competed in Jimmy Kimmel's Funniest College Student contest and from there was hooked on performing. Look for Bear Cave Comedy at anywhere from 6-10 pop-up comedy events along the central coast, expanding to the tri-state region.

Sam Bear launched her company, Bear Cave Productions, LLC in 2020 and has never looked back. She's used her company as an umbrella to pursue many business launches in varying directions. She does not subscribe to the entrepreneur title, and instead calls herself a "multiprenuer", integrating the lesson her mother imparted to her - of multiple streams of income - into her business model.

With a Master's in Behavior Change from the University of Kentucky, Sam excels as a Comedy Coach, Public Speaker, and Comedian. Through her comedy coaching, she guides clients in conquering imposter syndrome and stepping wholeheartedly into their sense of self.

# MORE FEMALE HEADLINERS: APPLY WITHIN

By Samantha Bearman

People always ask me how I started getting into stand-up comedy, and the truth of it is I have always loved making people laugh. I would tell jokes at the dinner table, and whenever I saw a stranger paying attention to a silly voice I was doing in public, I would always ham it up and exaggerate my movements. Out of the corner of my eye, I'd watch in delight as the passerby would smile and laugh. A thrill for my parents I'm sure. Despite never making it onto my high school improv team, and after several years of tryouts for my college team, the allure of comedy and making people laugh was something I always chased. I was actually very scared to switch from improv comedy, which is a team dynamic, to stand-up comedy, which relies solely on myself. I worried whether I would be able to captivate an audience and get them to laugh with just jokes I wrote instead of working with a group of comedy performers who work together to make each other shine. I would be the deciding factor in if I soared or if my jokes bombed. I signed up for a comedy writing workshop that had a guaranteed showcase following graduation. I knew that if I put my money where my mouth was there would be no turning back. I approached the workshop with absolute seriousness, took notes, wrote jokes, revised jokes, wrote bridges and transitions, and practiced for hours the week leading up to the performance. The night of the showcase I was able to feel an energy that I only got in moments and glimpses throughout my improv group performances. I felt electric and completely energized by being able to make people laugh; it felt like the ultimate superpower.

As I continued to pursue comedy and performed in more shows, I quickly noticed that most comedy shows tend to lean more towards all male lineups, and the struggle for a woman of color is tenfold harder. There is so much gatekeeping within the comedy industry, it feels like the Wild Wild West with simultaneously no rules and yet inundated with a myriad of unspoken rules that are frankly outdated. When I first started my comedy career, I had big dreams of running a successful club. Everywhere I looked were stories of men dominating the stage time and women struggling to break through the glass ceiling that seemed impenetrable.

But then something shifted inside me and I decided that enough was enough - it was time for me to take action. As I started taking my comedy career more seriously, I began to champion the belief that women deserve a right to stage time without having to compromise. I used to walk past buildings for rent and dream about what my comedy club would look like. I knew the name of it immediately, "The Bear Cave". It took about a year of walking past empty buildings for me to realize that I was building a story around a limiting belief that I created that I was not able to run a comedy business without a brick-and-mortar. And so, armed with a newfound sense of determination and ambition, I began searching for venues where female comics could have their own space to share their talents without having to compromise or settle for second-class status. The moment I shifted gears and opened my eyes up to a different way of accomplishing the same goal, opportunities began to present themselves. In the words of my mother, "Risk is the price of admission."

Now to be clear, this isn't a Cinderella story where in one night my entire life was changed. In all honesty, my first venue took over one year to secure, which included so many follow-ups, projections, circling back, and site visits I had almost lost faith. However, when I was given the green light, it all paid off because I had sold out shows for my first three shows - and then the world shut down. I remember during each sold-out show, feeling such a sense of pride as I thought to myself, "This is going to work!" Looking out at the packed venue, where people were careening their necks just to get even an obstructed view of the stage to now, suddenly, being stuck at home, with packed rooms being the scariest place to be. The week of the shutdown was different for everyone. I was excited to be going into my fourth month producing pop-up comedy shows at a great venue and anticipating another sold-out attendance. Then suddenly people started calling in asking for a refund, or if they could use their ticket for another night. The venue continued to assure me if people had tickets they would still allow and encourage the show. All of my comedians called and texted ferociously confirming that this show was still happening, as their packed calendars had become completely sparse of shows within days. Then it happened - the global shutdown and state of emergency notice on March 13th, 2020. It was as if everything I could see in the future vanished before it had really grown legs.

So how did I get started? It began when I believed that I had a right to exist within the comedy scene. However, to get to the true nitty-gritty of how I got started we have to go back to March of 2020 when the world stopped. It would only take two months after the world shut down for me to experience being furloughed and having to apply for unemployment for the first time in my entire life. I remember being angry, and for the first time in my life at a complete loss for words. I went home and I cried. I cried for two days. I kept thinking that all of the security that I had built, the traditional path I had followed, was just taken away from me. I felt frustrated and helpless in the situation. I had been temporarily deemed an essential worker and felt so grateful to have a job when so many people around me, through no fault of their own, had no source of income, and then just like that I was in the same boat as them. However, ever the pragmatic optimist and with a mother who is a career counselor who always was able to help people explain gaps in their resumes, I decided that honestly, now was as good a time as any to take chances! I embarked on the greatest risk of my life and bet everything on myself and this idea to bring comedy back to the central coast. And thus, Bear Cave Productions was born. Now it is important to note that in a beautiful twist of universal fate, the day that I was furloughed happened to fall on my last meeting with my business coach. I had been laying the groundwork for three months prior to launching into the world of entrepreneurship. While I had intended for the transition to be slow and steady, the universe, as she often does, had other plans.

Throughout my business endeavors and entrepreneurial pursuits I had to tackle a significant amount of imposter syndrome. I had swirling thoughts constantly coming to the forefront of my brain. What gave me the right to start my own comedy show? How would I be able to attract large names in the comedy industry to my stage? How would I be able to create an environment that fostered community and facilitated an eclectic array of voices and points of view on my stage? On top of realizing I have imposter syndrome to contend with, I also have ADHD and am healing from codependency, which means that I'm also a people pleaser in recovery. All this to say that my neurodivergent brain is one of my greatest assets in building my revenue streams and is also something that I have to constantly aim at working with instead of working against. All the notebooks and well-intentioned planning do nothing when decision paralysis sets in. I decided having questions was really good, but having answers wasn't necessary for continuing to have forward momentum. I decided I would figure it out as I went along, and if I didn't figure it out then it wasn't important for me to find the answer at that moment in time. You'd be surprised how much you can accomplish when you give yourself permission to move forward without a roadmap and create a map that ebbs and flows and changes based on your needs, your wants, and your ability to pay for somebody else to do the parts of your job that you'd rather not do.

One of my greatest inspirations for starting my business was the lack of representation that I continue to see on comedy show after comedy show after comedy show. Countless shows packed with men and only men, shows that had stacked lineups of only cis, white, heterosexual men prattling off their jokes (albeit some incredibly well crafted) only presented the audience with one point of view. I wanted to hear jokes and stories from women, from people of color, from the LGBTQ+ community, from older comedians well into their 60s, and fresh-faced comedians who are 19 and trying to sneak their way into a comedy club or nightclub to tell their jokes. I wanted to create an environment where the audience could find something in common with a person on stage who looked nothing like them and had walked a completely different life. This was what really led to the creation of my business motto which is, "Come for the Comedy and stay for the Community." It is important to understand that wishing will not make it so. There are many rules that we set for ourselves and believe them to be operating truths in the world. When in reality, these are made-up rules that we think we have to follow in order to do something the right way. I challenge you to be inspired, and instead of waiting around until someone gives you permission or approval to realize your dream, opt to take matters into your own hands. The stage is waiting for you!

## Lorena Coreas

Creative Entrepreneur

www.linkedin.com/in/lorena-coreas
https://www.instagram.com/lorena.p.coreas/

Lorena Coreas, the new voice of the hood, is a self-proclaimed fitness aficionado from the ghettos of downtown Los Angeles who laughs at inappropriate times and fantasizes about sleeping. Lorena is a vivacious, up-and-coming author and prospective business owner whose work has been featured on the Huffington Post and a beer website you've probably never heard of. She is the author of several memoirs from her various lives and an Old Hollywood-themed collection of LA Dodgers fanfiction "Mookie and the Three Sisters", which she insists is "sure to be my seminal work". It is exciting to see a fresh face so full of promise in the literary world- her passions include facetious witticism, physical well-being, serving others, and personal growth.

# A VIKING FUNERAL

By Lorena Coreas

Imagine putting all your shit into a canoe and letting it burn. Dressed in all black, shades to cover the glint in your eye. This isn't a sad occasion. It's badass. As badass as you are walking away from the wreckage as the flames illuminate behind you (imagine this in slow motion - just humor me). What's in your canoe? A sucky job, a failed relationship, all those books you swore to read but never did, the crafty Pinterest boards of the person you wish you were, or the embarrassment of that one time you thought a cute boy was waving at you but he was actually looking right past you. These moments have shaped the way we feel about ourselves, the way we move and make decisions.

Sometimes, and too often, we hang on to these identities that served previous versions of ourselves. The people we were when we were 15, then 21, then 25, then 30. And we carry that shit around like we're proud of it. We don't stop to admit that maybe there's a better way. We go through the same seasons of life over and over again; we call it a pattern. Maybe that's just because sometimes it's hard to learn. We see the math problem but we don't pause to solve it. What can we do to cleanse ourselves of these bad habits? Instead of just seeing them, calling them out, and chugging along. The fun part is that we're allowed to host ourselves a Viking funeral at any point we want. Figuratively, of course. And also literally if you have a permit, probably.

Being the daughter of an immigrant and having learned the English language at a young age, I became everything for my mom. I was her educator teaching her how to navigate her day-to-day responsibilities by learning those responsibilities myself and then translating them to her. I was her voice in the heat of any battle. I was her administrative assistant, making phone calls and filling out paperwork. At times this felt so tedious and exhausting. I was a child managing the duties of adult life. It might have felt annoying at the time, but it's a time I'm truly grateful for. It taught me how to handle business at a young age. It taught me to be adaptable so I could communicate with anyone we ran into and under any circumstance. I didn't realize how incredibly valuable that experience would be. When I joined the workforce I was so well-spoken and tactful that it helped me nail every interview I've ever had. Those interviews led to cool experiences in different jobs. I was organized and resourceful, setting me up to get the job done and done well. All along the way I was shaping myself to be a businesswoman, knowing how to handle myself with the utmost professional confidence.

Along with all of the cool skills I picked up as a kid, I also picked up some bad habits. Frustration when things didn't work the way they needed to. Impatience when we needed something and it was taking too long. Pride when I was challenged and needed to come out on top. That's why, as part of my career, my years of freelance writing were some of my favorite professionally. Being a finance girl for the majority of my career, it felt so refreshing to allow my creativity to flow for the first time. This burst of creativity spoke life into other areas of my life too. My relationship and my friendships, my motherhood, my solitude- it was powerful in transforming who I was in every aspect of my life. A phoenix rising high against the flames and reborn majestically. It was stripping away the cloudiness that was keeping me from emerging.

That drove me to do more in my career. My career was stable and it felt safe. My performance spoke for itself and it gained me promotion after promotion. I was moving up the corporate ladder. This is where the ugly pride came in. I wasn't used to a challenge, so facing one just made me annoyed and angry. Somehow, I convinced myself that with all my accomplishments I was just too good to be put through any challenge. When in reality, it was all my fear of failure. It was more important to feel good about myself than to be faced with my shortcomings, so instead I just tried to ignore them. That obviously didn't serve me well because pretty soon I wasn't moving forward in my career anymore. I was in a role as a purchasing manager leading a team at a major Fortune 500 company, and honestly, just eating dirt every day. My only defense is that this department was antiquated and used manual processes that they just refused to automate. They were scared of change and I was scared of failing, so when the manual processes were making things way too complicated, my pride got in the way and I blamed it on all of them. I'd roll my eyes at their click counters and dilapidated paper filing and condescendingly campaigned for automated processes.

I was so caught up in getting them to do things my foolproof way that I was hurting myself by not slowing down to learn things their way. I had given up on their processes and pushed past them to do things how I wanted to. Any guesses on whether or not that worked out? It did not. I decided the job wasn't the right fit and was eventually promoted. The wisdom comes in hindsight knowing that if I had just worked with what I had instead of insisting I could do it better on my own, we could have been a successful partnership, and the trust that I would have built would have granted me the improvements I so desperately wanted to make. My pride was just too inflated to let me see that I was misbehaving. I'm just gonna say it - I was throwing a fit.

I guess I always thought I was a patient person. And to some degree, I am, just not when it comes to my career. I always wanted more and more. I was obnoxiously restless, so eager and excited to learn something new, which sounds like a good thing, but it manifested itself as impatience. I moved into each new role with excitement, feeling like I could take on the world, but that delusion ran me into a brick wall. I started to realize that my impatience was pointing out that I was not doing anything I actually wanted to do; nothing that I had a true desire for. I was impatient because I simply didn't care for it, so I just kept moving on to the next thing. In a weird way, it served me well because I had a healthy career, but it also meant that I was digging deeper into something I had no passion for. I was sick of working on everybody else's goals and finally wanted to work on something of my own.

This inability to wait forced my hand and I ended up quitting my fancy, new national sales manager job. Most patient, well-behaved adults would have put a plan into place so they could get their affairs in order, but my stubborn ass wanted things my way and wanted them right now. This new phase of my professional life won't have as much room for impatience. It's going to require a lot of patience. I'm currently working for myself and freelancing again. I'm training to become a fitness leader which will lead to other opportunities I'm going to create for myself. I'm wise enough now to know that patience is going to be my best friend. She's going to teach me everything I need to know and take me step by step so that the empire I have in mind comes to life. All in due time.

This season of purging has honestly been my favorite so far. I'm getting to see myself with fresh eyes and a translucency I've never experienced before. It's like opening the blinds and getting to see all the dusty corners so you can clean them out. You feel like you can breathe a little easier. As I self-reflect and slowly walk around my heart and mind, picking up the bad habits I finally realized were there and organizing the clutter left behind from my ill-informed decisions and tossing them in my canoe, I look forward to making space for the wisdom, clarity, and confidence that will drive me closer to my goals. My canoe is getting filled to the brim with all those useless things that I stupidly tried to hang on to. Lighting the matches (or maybe I need a blowtorch) and letting it float away. Remember to throw a Viking funeral as often as you need to. Sometimes you just gotta let that shit go up in flames.

## Jasmin Valdez

Founder of Modern Mindset Movement

www.facebook.com/allthingsjazziv
https://www.instagram.com/jasmin.e.valdez
www.modernmindsetmovement.com
apply.modernmindsetmovement.com

Jasmin is a first-generation Latina business coach who has helped and inspired hundreds of women across the world to take action toward achieving their goals. As a first-time mom, she is on a journey to help other moms find the freedom to spend time at home with their families while providing for them. She focuses on helping other women break generational cycles, healing their inner child, and becoming financially free.

# SHE'S SO, COMO SE DICE... LUCKY!

## By Jasmin Valdez

Before I jump into my life and how I help others, I want to take some time to explain how I got here, which arguably is the most important part. Oftentimes, you see successful people and think, "wow they're so lucky" or "wow they must have had it easy." It's hard to see successful people and think, "wow they went through so many hard times to get there". So let's go over this "luck" of mine that people seem to think got me here.

Picture a tiny town of only 8,000 people in the middle of nowhere. That's where my story began, in good old Lexington, Nebraska (bonus points if you can show me where that is on the map).

I should mention that my mom immigrated there from Guatemala. This naturally meant that my mom, who single-handedly raised my three siblings and me, struggled to speak English. Which meant she was limited in the jobs she could work at. It also meant that due to financial hardships, we could only afford to live in a small apartment where I shared a bed with my mom and sister up until I left for college.

For most of my life, I remember my mom working at a factory where she worked over 60 hours weekly and only got one day off a week, only to receive a $600 paycheck. On her day off, she would clean and cook all day long. The same goes for when she would come home from work after a long day. She never complained or showed signs that it was stressful. She made it look so easy. I now realize it was anything but easy.

Throughout most of my high school experience, I wore a lot of hats. I was the interpreter for my mom when it came to legal documents or just checking out at a grocery store. I also wore the hats of the big sister, multi-passionate overachiever, and most importantly, the daughter who was "supposed" to go to college and get her education.

All these put a large weight on my teenage shoulders which only led me to toughen up and mature early for my age. Not to mention I was one of the oldest in my grade, so naturally everyone always told me I was mature for my age. They didn't know it was just childhood traumas that caused that maturity.

Over the course of a few years, so many things happened that it's all a blur to me now. I went from experiencing my mom getting deported back to Guatemala to getting accepted into a scholarship program that would pay for my full tuition to get my bachelor's degree and getting accepted into college. Then I was moving out of my hometown, attending college as a minority in a campus that was primarily white, graduating with my Bachelor's in Business Management, and getting hired into an executive management role in retail that same week. Phew, that was a LOT, and it all went by so fast!

Oh, and somewhere in all the madness I met my lifelong partner who has been my biggest cheerleader since then.

So you must be thinking, ok but what does that have to do with where you are now?

EVERYTHING.

If it weren't for my experiences of growing up in a low-income household, facing adversity, and having to be resilient, I wouldn't be where I'm at today. Which is why you're here, reading this chapter now.

Did I mention I have a son now? Whoa. As if my life hadn't taken so many turns, this one took the cake.

Having my son at 26, I had a huge mindset shift. I no longer wanted to climb the corporate ladder. I no longer wanted to have a "big girl" job that kept me away from him for over 50 hours a week. So how did I get here? It wasn't working in retail management, I'll tell you that much.

When he was born, I made a promise that he would never live a childhood like mine. He would never experience what it was like to be struggling financially, growing up in a cramped, bed bug-infested apartment. I refused to let my son grow up saying, "I wish my mom wasn't always working" or,"I wish we could take vacations like my friends do" or, "I wish we had money to buy that toy."

I knew I was meant for more and, just like my mom, worked hard to give us the life I always dreamed of for my family.

When leaving the corporate world, which was a whole journey in itself, I never envisioned myself leaving the career I thought was going to be a part of my life forever. As a new mom who was looking to spend more time at home with her son, I did what any other mom would do - I started searching the internet for work-from-home jobs.

Talk about disappointment! The amount of jobs that offered flexible schedules to fit a mom's lifestyle was practically zero. I didn't want a job that would require my attention 40 hours a week because that would mean I would've given up about 37,560 hours until he turned 18. Absolutely not; no mom should ever have to do that. As a mom, we're expected to choose between family time and income, and I refused to make that my reality.

So, then what? What is a mom looking to stay home and be present supposed to do to provide for her family? It wasn't clear at first, but after looking more into starting my own business, I knew that was the right answer.

Was it scary to do something outside my comfort zone? Absolutely. Did I doubt myself and my business several times throughout the process? You bet. Would I do it all over again? 100%.

I wanted to create a space where I could mentor other moms who found themselves in my position: to create an income from home while still being present. I was tired of seeing women in any industry not earn their worth on top of drowning in money-related misery. So I took a leap of faith and soon after I realized this was exactly what I was meant to be doing all along.

As I am writing this, my son is almost two years old and living in a newly constructed home (the type of home I used to dream of), with his very own room and bed, where we get to travel more than I ever did growing up. Best of all, we get to hang out every single day as a family.

The best part about all of this is that I have now been able to help so many women across the world do exactly what I did and create an automated income online from the comfort of their homes. What does that mean? Well, I coach women in starting their own high-ticket affiliate sales businesses. I work one-on-one with them to guide them through the process and also show them what is possible with an automated business.

Having automation in place means that there are business tasks that are running in the background while I actually spend time with my son. It means I can wake up and see notifications on my phone of commissions hitting my bank account without having to be glued to my phone or computer to generate income.

Seeing other women step into the online space and place their trust in me is more than I could ever ask for. I knew I always wanted to inspire and motivate other people, but I never knew this was the path I was meant for until I had my son.

When it comes to people seeing my success now and saying, "wow you're so lucky" or "wow you must've had help from your parents", I can't help but laugh. There's so much to me that people don't know about, there are so many tears and stress that led me to where I am today, that now YOU know about. So, I guess looking back on all of it, I AM lucky.

I'm so lucky to have struggled in my childhood. I'm so lucky to have faced so many hardships that created my drive to create the life of my dreams. The rest? That was all hard work.

Now that you've gotten a chance to hear about my story, I'd love to end with some tips for women looking to achieve the lifestyle I've been able to create for my family.

**Tip #1:** Write down your goals. The two most important points on a map are where you're currently at and where you're going. Writing down your goals and creating a game plan will help create your roadmap to success.

**Tip #2:** Learn something new every day. As a mom, it's so hard to live the same day over and over. The last thing you want is to let five years go by and realize you haven't moved forward in life or gotten closer to your goals. Make sure to set aside 30 minutes every day to learn something new whether that's through a podcast, a book, or someone you know. Small progress every day adds up quickly.

**Tip #3:** Find a Mentor. As someone who thought I could figure out everything on my own, I'm here to tell you that it's so much faster to lean on the knowledge of others! That's where I come in. As a current business mentor, I help collapse the timelines of moms looking to achieve their dream lives. Not to mention the average millionaire had seven mentors before earning their first million.

I hope my story resonated with you and allowed you to see that if I could make it to my dream life, you can too. I'm looking forward to working with even more ambitious women looking to make a change. If that is you, you can find me on Instagram at @jasmin.e.valdez or at www.modernmindsetmovement.com.

## Gabby Gutierrez

The beauty of success by Gabby G
Inspirational, motivational life and business coach
and a Brand Ambassador

http://www.linkedin.com/in/gabby-gutierrez-b16ab736
https://www.facebook.com/gabby.gutierrez.9081
https://www.instagram.com/gabbygu9/
https://thebeautyofsuccess.com/

I'm Gabby Gutierrez, a passionate and determined woman, who has taken all her experiences in life and turned them into helping and supporting people to reach their full potential, find a purpose, and live happier lives.

I have been working and influencing thousands of women as an entrepreneur for the last 30 years, reaching one of the top positions in the company I represent. My passion for personal development has me always looking for new ways to help others. ♥

# FROM DREAMER TO ENTREPRENEUR

## By Gabby Gutierrez

This time, I'm not going to start with my whole life story – that would be too long. Life is truly strange; it leads us down different paths. Sometimes, we don't understand where it's taking us. We need to listen a lot and trust the process, understanding that the only thing we need to do is keep moving forward. This can be challenging because many times, the path in front of us is not clear.

I was a college student in Mexico who decided to study psychology. However, after a few semesters, God had a different plan for me, and I had to move to the United States, putting my dream of becoming a clinical psychologist on hold. Once in the new country, I tried a few times to continue my career, but every time I resumed my classes something in my life interfered, and I had to put my schooling on hold again and again.

I always said that I was not a good salesperson and that I didn't like sales at all. Have you ever felt like you don't want to do something, but life pushes you down that path anyway? Life and God had a plan for me, and I had no idea how my life would turn around.

Who could have told me at that time that the decision I took - temporarily joining a cosmetic company - would become my career and my passion for three decades of my life?

Something that I've learned during my 30 years of experience in the sales and leadership field while working and helping people find their passion and purpose, is that when you have a dream in your heart and you feel that there is more out there (I'm not just talking about material things but everything in your life), you have to pay attention to your gut feeling. Your heart and soul know that you were born to achieve more.

Like every business one starts, mine was not an easy process. I had to navigate through many challenging situations. In addition to dealing with fear and doubt, I also had to relocate from one state to another. This new location was not only unfamiliar but also far away from my family and friends. Starting in a new city where I only knew one person, I once again questioned myself: was this the right decision? Because something didn't feel right, and things were not progressing in the direction I had planned.

One of the things I learned at that moment was that we are not trees; we are not rooted in one place. Thanks to God, we can move, and there's nothing wrong with that. If you're not happy and something inside is telling you that there's more out there for you, and you feel you're not in the right place, good news! You CAN MOVE!!!

I had read and listened to a lot about how decisions shape our destiny. At that time, I didn't fully understand it, but now, at this mature stage of life, I can see how life continually presents us with decisions to either change or enhance our lives. However, it all depends on us, because many things we desire lie outside of our comfort zone.

After a few months in that new place, life once again compelled me to move, this time even further north from where I had been. However, this time, the place I chose truly brought me happiness. I felt it was the right place, and I wasn't wrong; it was indeed the right place.

I cherished everything about this new location – the scenery, the people, the weather – EVERYTHING. Now, I understand the importance of following your gut feeling. I firmly believe that our hearts always know, but many times, we ignore it and try to silence its call.

It was the place I chose, or better yet, the place God chose for me to pursue my dreams. I had a clear vision of what I wanted to achieve, but I was heartbroken. Here, once again, another lesson was learned: we have the option to let the things that happen destroy us or make us stronger. Have you ever heard that phrase that says to "send your heart and your dream to the front, and your body will follow"? Well, that's exactly what I did. Now I know that when the heart and mind work together, they are a powerful force.

When you know what you WANT, when you have it really CLEAR, when you place it in your HEART first and can feel it, then you put it in your MIND, the "how" and "what to do" will begin to appear like a bridge being built in front of you as you walk.

In my life, I've had to face numerous challenging situations. You might be thinking at this moment, "Yes, but you're not dealing with the problem or situation I'm facing." I always respond to that with a smile and say, "If I were to share my story, you might find yourself shedding tears with me." I've learned to practice resilience and understand that when we encounter difficult situations, they are not permanent. If we confront them and learn from them, we grow stronger and stronger. Remember, pain is inevitable, but suffering is optional.

One of the lessons I've learned from dealing with problems is not to remain stagnant. If it hurts, we need to move, take action, seek support, and never give up on ourselves. Always remember your worth.

Now, let me revisit the story of the beginning of my business and how it rapidly grew, achieving one goal after another. Initially, I was searching for a way to meet my financial needs so I could quit the two jobs I had at the time. I had a clear goal of attaining both financial and time freedom.

One of the most crucial things to understand when starting a business is that most of the time, you'll face rejection more often than acceptance. However, it's through these experiences that we can improve and become better at what we do.

If you have experienced rejection, or if someone has told you, "You're dreaming, wake up!"—CONGRATULATIONS. That means you've already taken the first steps to moving forward.

Believe it or not, as I received "Nos" and faced rejection in my late 20s, my passion and energy increased. I didn't know or fully understand the HOW at that time, but my WHAT and WHY were crystal clear.

As I began to expand my business, my team was also simultaneously growing theirs. It was during this period that I grasped the importance of focusing on helping and serving others, which results in rewards multiplying exponentially. In less than a year and a half, I found myself enjoying the highest positions within the company. At that time, I wasn't fully aware of how much I had achieved. However, what I can tell you is that PASSION, combined with MASSIVE ACTIONS and EXCELLENT SERVICE, always brings remarkable rewards.

I have held the top position in the company for the past 13 years and had the privilege of enjoying numerous wonderful experiences. During this time, I've had the opportunity to help, support, and inspire thousands of women to improve their self-esteem, lead happier lives, dream big, and achieve their goals.

When you achieve your goals, it's common to lose focus because you've already attained what you desire. However, the truth is that achieving a dream is not the ultimate goal; achieving a goal is just a moment. The most crucial aspect is the person you become in the process. That's why, if you achieve a goal and don't have a new one ready, you'll eventually lose momentum and find yourself slipping into a comfort zone. As an entrepreneur or business owner, it's important to always measure your results, continue to grow, and consistently set new goals.

We are in a new era where we have digital tools and knowledge at our fingertips. However, we also face a significant challenge – we tend to compare ourselves to others more than ever. Sometimes, this self-comparison leads to self-doubt, paralysis, and an unhealthy pursuit of perfection over progress.

It's crucial to seek out role models and mentors because there's always someone who has achieved what you aspire to. These individuals can help you save time and learn from their experiences. Remember, we are constantly on a learning journey that never truly ends. Keep your mind open, as everyone has something valuable to teach us.

Always remember that you are UNIQUE, and there is no one quite like you. God has bestowed upon your talents and gifts to fulfill the dreams He has placed in your heart. You have a purpose; don't leave this life without accomplishing it.

I hope my brief story encourages, serves, or inspires you. Wishing you the very best from the bottom of my heart,

Gabby Gutierrez

## Julissa Sanchez

Julissa Sanchez Consulting

www.linkedin.com/in/julissa-sanchez-72414394
https://www.facebook.com/profile.php?id=100070802171018
https://www.instagram.com/huitzin_julissa/

Julissa Sánchez is a fierce mujer, Xicana Sinaloense, originally from Los Angeles, who grew up along the West Coast. She is mothering the revolution. An activist and community organizer, supporting the liberation of her people through policy, culture, healing, and her writing. Her passion for culture, decolonization, and social justice led her to study Latin American Studies with a minor in Human Rights at the University of Washington. As a dedicated advocate for youth, cultural education, language, housing, and racial justice, her work is focused on community-led organizing based on self-empowerment, anti-displacement, anti-racism, and advocacy centered around language justice.

She is currently working on her first novel based on a true story of miracles. Julissa is passionate about writing as a form of self-expression and believes in the power of owning one's narratives. Her writing is focused on lived experience, hoping to inspire mujeres to own their stories, and power and live their truths.

# WE ALL DREAM IN DIFFERENT LANGUAGES

By Julissa Sanchez

My mom waited impatiently for me to translate to her what a document from the court said. I could understand most of the words the court document said in English, but how could I translate these big words I hardly knew in English into Spanish? I was just a young girl still learning the language myself.

English is my second language. Even though I was born in the United States, I didn't truly learn English until I moved to Seattle from Los Angeles in the mid-90s. I was in ESL (English Secondary Language) classes until I was in the seventh grade. My mother who hardly spoke English always asked me to translate important medical, legal, and business documents for her. Some of the words I didn't understand; however, I tried as much as I could.

"Y para qué vas a la escuela?" (What do you go to school for?) My mom would respond angrily to my loss of words.

I wonder how much important information was lost in translation.

Decades later I am sitting across from a Latina woman who was very nervous due to the notice to vacate she got from her landlord. She didn't speak English and needed help understanding what the notice meant. It was like I was that little girl again, staring into my mother's worried eyes hoping to get guidance from me. This time though, I was fluent in English and Spanish, and held a Bachelor of Arts in Latin American Studies with a minor in Human Rights, from the University of Washington.

Working for human rights has always been a passion of mine. I was fortunate enough to start my work in housing justice soon after college. Here, I noticed a gap between housing justice resources and the Latino community. Sure, the Tenant's Rights Hotline had interpretation on demand, yet very few Latino tenants called the hotline.

It came down to two important matters: language and cultural relevance. Without these two factors, it is difficult for Latino tenants to trust organizations, know where to access resources about their rights, or know what rights they have. This is especially true for undocumented tenants.

Decentralizing English became my main goal in my housing justice work.

Creating a Know Your Rights workshop in Spanish was the first step to building the bridge between the tenant rights resources and the Latino community. As an outreach strategy to inform the Latinx community of this resource in their language, I partnered with key stakeholders and organizations around the region that served the Latino community and whom the Latino community trusted.

Community needs and interest made the workshops popular; I was no longer only giving presentations to tenants in buildings. Organizations that served the Latino community like El Centro de La Raza, the University of Washington, the City of Seattle, and Univision frequently invited me to facilitate workshops and training on tenants' rights for their employers.

For many years the city of Seattle has been gentrified and much of the Latinx community has been pushed out to the cities south of King County. Unfortunately, many of these cities do not have strong tenant protections. It was common for landlords to give 20-day, no-cause eviction notices to tenants in retaliation when tenants would demand their rights to repairs, or simply because of discrimination.

Often the Latino tenants who do not speak English do not understand these notices, and get really intimidated and all too often taken advantage of. The language barrier often leaves tenants intimidated when they receive a vacate notice, believing they must vacate within 20 days. Many times, they do not know where to turn or who to contact. This is a huge problem, as it leaves tenants vulnerable to further financial hardships, displacement, or homelessness.

Understanding the urgency of this matter, I established the first bilingual tenant's rights clinic in the city of Burien, a city in King County with a 23% Latino population. The clinic prioritized the Spanish speakers; however, we served all tenants in south King County. It's important to note that I didn't just provide information about tenant rights, as information alone can be daunting when navigating systems and paperwork in English. Especially with tenant protections that are self-enforceable. The clinic supported tenants with case management, guidance, mediation between landlord and tenant, and culturally relevant communication in Spanish. Beyond language, there is a certain comfort and trust in speaking to someone who is from your community and culturally connected.

Knowing their tenant rights empowered Latino tenants to organize for better living conditions in their buildings, to stand up for their rights and their deposit refunds, and to fight unlawful evictions.

Language justice goes beyond Spanish of course. A true highlight of the language justice program was when the P'urhépecha community invited me to give a Know Your Rights (KYR) presentation during which an elder translated from Spanish into P'urhépecha (a Mexican indigenous language).

In response to the COVID-19 crisis, which shook the world in unimaginably devastating ways, I launched the KYR Hotline exclusively in Spanish. Latino tenants who worked in the service industry, such as restaurants and hotels, found themselves unable to go to work. The dire need for information and advocacy around tenant rights during the pandemic was so vast, that my number to the hotline reached Chicago and different cities across California.

Furthermore, I advocated for prioritizing the implementation of language justice in the Tenants Union organization. I pushed for making the translation and interpretation budget higher. Any webinar that the Tenants Union facilitated was completely bilingual. If you weren't bilingual, especially if you only spoke English, you had to sign up for interpretation. My advocacy for language justice went as far as city councils, pushing city council members to interpret the city council meeting so their Spanish-speaking constituents felt included and were also a part of the matters being voted on that affected their livelihoods.

When it was time to leave the Tenants Union, there was still a great deal of visioning and work left to be done in the language justice program. I was inspired to start a consulting business to support my vision of language justice being centered as a part of social justice frameworks in nonprofit organizations, as well as for corporations that want to grow in their diversity, equity, and inclusion efforts. We must ask ourselves, is it serving justice if an organization's or company's services are inaccessible to communities directly impacted by language and cultural barriers?

Language access is regularly forgotten as a need for people, including in social justice spaces. All too often, I must ask event planning committees what their plan for language justice is. I am almost always given a confused and hesitant response. All too often, people whose language is not English have not been given a spot at the table or even been considered. Even when a city council is voting on important matters that will affect non-English speakers' lives. Or when a community organizing events are being held that claim to stand for equity and inclusion, or when there is a survey for improving living conditions or attempting to gather information on experiences with discrimination without creating a safe space for non-English speakers. My work centers people who speak Spanish and the critical thought of planning around making spaces inclusive for people to feel comfortable to express themselves in their own languages, in their culture.

The Latino community has expressed that they do not feel welcomed or safe to express their lived experiences or opinions or get services at places where they are made to feel second-class when their voices are not being centered.

My leadership centers on undocumented, immigrant, and Latina women to strengthen their empowerment through language justice. Women have been the ones leading their families' efforts to get housing justice. The language justice I helped establish empowered women to go to courts despite their immigrant status to fight for their deposits; it empowered women to fight against unlawful evictions. And they won. It has empowered women to organize their communities for better living conditions. Making spaces for voices to be heard in the language they dream in has made women feel heard and motivated to speak up about what matters the most to them. The best advice I can give other women is to use their stories and their passions, and create them into their purpose, to inspire themselves and others.

With that, I would like to leave you all with a sample of my passion and purpose which is to use the languages I dream in to tell stories, and share with you an excerpt of my novel that will be coming soon:

Paramedics attempted to keep the girl conscious.

But it was in vain.

The celestial light in the girl's green eyes dimmed by the second.

Her spirit deliberately streamed out of her body, into the gentle embrace *de la Muerte*.

Valentina found comfort in *La Muerte's* familiar cold apapacho.
memories ancient as time
past
present
future
eternal
all one
memories older than I
ancient ones
all a part of me
Memories

Pitch blackness.
I opened my eyes to a darkness with a mixed scent of dirt, flowers, and herbs.
A heartbeat sang at the same rhythm as mine.
My spirit stretched out of the fetal position it lay on.

A small orange flame ignited from the ground.
illuminating the colorful darkness

Stars started falling from the sky, in the form of ancient ones.
Making a circle around the fire.
An ancient one, with a moon face the color of the earth, high cheekbones, with long black braids, squeezed my cheeks.
Que bonita mi niña she said proudly.
Abuela Lupa?! I gasped!
Abuela Lupa was the mother of my maternal abuelo Beto. I got to meet my great grand abuela Lupa a few times before she passed away.
The ancient one chuckled. "Ven, sit down with us." she said in a gentle voice. There is so much we need to catch up on.
Around the fire sat ancient ones she didn't know, but somehow felt so familiar.

Abuela Lupa, am I dead? I hesitantly asked.

Before I could get any answers, the flames magnified.

Within the fire a portal opened to a memory of a distant time; a distant place.

## Samantha Holm

CEO of Miss Sam & Atlas Beauty

https://www.facebook.com/xomisssam/
https://www.instagram.com/xomisssam/
https://misssambeauty.com/

Samantha Holm is a Permanent Makeup Artist and Salon Owner in Eastern Washington State. She has been in business since 2016 and opened her salon in October 2020 during the height of the pandemic. She is also an educator and business coach who loves sharing how life-changing it is to start your own business. She has a huge passion for life and wants to inspire others to live their ultimate dream lives. She is married to the love of her life, Mike, and is a dog mom to two adorable puppies, Mylo and Sven.

# THANKS TO HER

## By Samantha Holm

What if I told you that I went against everything that was expected of me? That I went against what was supposed to be the "norm" and said not just NO to everything that was supposed to be the "norm", but said, "fuck that shit." I knew the normal path of life was not for me. I knew I was meant for something bigger. I knew I had to create my new reality and make sure I was creating the best version of myself to obtain everything I ever wanted.

Societal expectations dictated that I should go to college, get a degree, marry young, be active in the church, and marry in the temple. It was apparent that I was not only supposed to have kids but also have a stable 9-5 corporate job and contribute to society. I was supposed to be modest, to just sit there, look pretty, and not make others feel uncomfortable. I laugh looking back on all those expectations because now I'm living the exact opposite, and I feel more like myself than ever.

It was the end of my final semester of college. I had just walked out of what would be my last class feeling bittersweet and so thankful that I had chosen to end my college career early. The funny thing is I always loved school, until college that is, and then it got extremely difficult. A lot of people won't tell you how drastically your life can change in just a few months. At the time, I was going to school for business, because ever since I was a little girl, I loved the idea of owning and running my own business.

I believe it was just a month or two after leaving school, I saw one of my friends post something on Facebook. She had just gotten certified in microblading eyebrows. I was genuinely so intrigued by it that I messaged her a few questions right away and she told me, "Sam, if you are so interested in it, I think you should take a class."

I impulsively pulled the trigger. I signed up for a class two weeks later and now here I am almost seven years into my career. It truly goes to show that some of the 'random' callings in life are not just random, sometimes they lead to new beginnings that can then become the catalyst for the rest of your life.

Six months after opening my business, my then fiancé, now husband, wanted to move back home to Washington State which was about 900 miles and a few states away from where we lived. I just remember being so ready for a change! I moved there with no job, no friends nor family, only with a dream and a prayer for a better life, and it was one of the best decisions we could've ever made.

Without hesitation, I started my business over again. I reached out to a few salons and found one that would work. While I built up my business and my clientele, I worked other jobs. Sometimes three jobs at a time, and I hustled to make my dream come true. There is and should be no shame in working other jobs as you are building up your dream life and business. IT TAKES TIME!!! It also takes a lot of grit and dedication. I wanted to be financially secure before I jumped all in. It definitely doesn't happen overnight that's for sure. I consistently worked three jobs from 2017-2020. It took me 3 years to finally go full-time in my business, only for, you guessed it, the world and consequently, my business, to shut down.

We all thought, "It's only going to be two weeks, right?" That turned into four months. During our shutdown, I rested and took a lot of time for myself, but I also dedicated a lot of time to online trainings, practice, product creation, and revamping my business on the back end. I tried to stay as positive as possible and continued to market my business regardless of being closed. I was able to create quite a lengthy waiting list for appointments, which would set me up for success when we were to reopen. I knew I had to work hard during the downtime in order to build on all of the behind-the-scenes tasks for my business. I look back at that time fondly because it really created a better future for me. I'm so thankful that I had the foresight to put in a lot of hard work during that uncertain time.

My business and I came back stronger than ever. We reopened in July 2020, and I knew with how booked out I was that it was time to find a different place to work. I started searching for studios and salons and even looked into a few spaces while we were shut down. I was determined. Sure enough, I got a message from a friend about a salon space that seemed perfect. It was a huge space! I wasn't sure if I was ready to be a salon owner with so many stylists working under me, but I knew it was a good opportunity, so I went all in. I signed a lease on my very own salon that September. I opened Atlas Beauty in October of 2020 and by April of 2021, six months after opening, I signed another lease to double the amount of space in my salon to further expand my business. This extra space would then allow me to start training, which is one of my true passions.

I did all of this despite the pandemic, despite the possibility of shutdowns, and everything fucking else. I went for it, and it turned out, again, to be one of the best decisions I ever made. I now have a team of 12 amazing women, and I am so blessed to have each of them be a part of my life.

That one decision has now opened up a myriad of opportunities for me and my business. At first, and honestly, for many years after I didn't receive a lot of support. A lot of people probably thought my job, my business, was a hobby, a side hustle, or if we are being real, they probably thought I was some dropout who just needed something to do.

Now, almost seven years into it, a lot of people probably still don't understand what I do to this day! And that's perfectly okay! I persevered anyway. I made a lot of friends and a lot of enemies, and I made a lot of them confused with everything that encompasses my business and life. I am the CEO of my own business which is such a weird thing to think about. Twenty-two-year-old me would be beyond proud of where our decisions got us to today. I encourage you to learn to love the journey. It's crazy, beautiful, and sometimes a heartbreakingly hard road, but I promise you it is beyond worth every minute. Just remember to stop and enjoy it, learn to laugh at yourself, and keep going.

The most difficult decision I ever had and have to make daily is whether or not to keep going or to quit. Both paths will hurt, but you have to choose which path is worth it. I obviously chose and continue to choose to keep going. Trust me, it wasn't all sunshine and roses. A lot of days, I wanted to quit. There was literally a lot of blood, sweat, and tears that went into this future I was building. Not everyone saw my vision, but I did, and that's all that mattered.

Something I personally have struggled with most of my life is getting over the hurdle of perfectionism. Wanting every aspect to be perfect, waiting for the perfect moment, time, and opportunity before I start something or do the thing I want to do. This has, in hindsight, crippled me and my growth both personally and professionally. I see this in so many others who struggle with this concept as well. Show up authentically and don't care about being perfect, take the messy action to get started. Too many people, dreams, ideas, and connections have died due to wanting and waiting for things to be perfect. Please do not fall victim to this idea of "perfect". Your life, your goals, and your dreams are too important and valuable to pass up.

I have vowed to myself to never give up on my plans and dreams for my life. I am so lucky to say that even being so young, I have knocked quite a few items off my bucket list. I'm so blessed and thankful for all the decisions my younger self made. My present self is so proud, thankful, and humbled. My past set me up for success, and I will continue to do that for my future self. I am ever-evolving, growing, learning on the go, and living for every moment of it!

Find the people who support you and hold them close. I am so thankful for the support of my husband. He has seen all sides of me and my crazy ideas and has been cheering me on for years. I know he just wants me to be happy, and sometimes my crazy, delusional decisions are what make me the happiest and have the biggest payoffs. We have had to find our own balance with managing my business, but overall, it has worked out well for us, our lifestyle, and our goals.

Looking back on my life, especially the last seven years, you could say that it seems we are all slightly delusional in the pursuit of our dreams in this thing we call life. Just remember we are all skeletons wearing meat suits living on a rock in the middle of a vast and amazing galaxy. Nothing is perfect and that is what makes this life so beautiful and interesting. Realizing that we are all perfectly imperfect beings, living right here, in this moment in time. Please remember this when you think of pursuing your dreams and goals. There is no limit. There is no cap. There is no dream or idea that is too big. If it does seem too big, chances are you just need to create the opportunity itself for it to come true.

So, I leave you with this: I hope you feel inspired to keep going. Regardless of if people are supporting you, regardless of whether it seems impossible or it seems hard. You've got you, and that's something worth betting on. Chase your dreams, laugh and cry along the way, and most importantly make a beautiful life that past, present, and future you would be proud of.

## Laura Miramontes

Break Free Counseling, LLC
Trauma Therapist, LMFT

https://www.linkedin.com/in/laura-miramontes-14a969249/
https://www.facebook.com/breakfreecounselingllc
https://www.instagram.com/breakfreecounseling/
www.breakfreecounseling.net

I am a therapist who is passionate about helping people reclaim their autonomy and identity an overall sense of freedom and happiness. I deeply understand the severe impacts of trauma and the value of safety and trust when processing and navigating the heavy emotions that can come from trauma.

One of my specialties is helping folks find healing and freedom from religious harm. I use warmth and unconditional acceptance to create a safe space for people to explore their experiences inside or outside their religious environment. I help them explore messages that are persistently taught or the interactions they have with the leader or people in authority. My experience in therapy and as a survivor of religious trauma allows me to understand the complexities and the meaning of trauma work.

# THE POWER OF BREAKING FREE: LETTING GO OF HIGH CONTROL RELIGION

By Laura Miramontes

## Vulnerabilities

I was in my early twenties, searching for a church. The place that had always given me a feeling of belonging and connection. I was searching for a new religion as my Catholic faith did not resonate with me anymore. I thought I would search for a non-Catholic Christian church where I did not have to confess sins to a priest or pray to saints, as I had felt praying to anyone but God was not allowing me to fully connect with God at the time.

I was living in Eugene, Oregon attending the University of Oregon to obtain my Master's in Couples and Family Therapy. I was feeling anxious and excited to start this new journey of learning how to be a therapist and help others navigate their relationships and mental health journeys. My search for belonging was important as I was unfamiliar with the new town, people, or school.

I hoped to find a church that spoke the "truth" of who God was as I was feeling lost in my connection with a higher power. I had no idea feeling lost would make me vulnerable to selecting a church with a leader whom I automatically trusted to teach me how to live my life.

I soon found a small church in Eugene a few minutes away from my apartment. I walked in and it felt familiar. It felt as if I was walking into a room of a large Latino family. They were happy to see a newcomer and greeted me with hugs and smiles. I felt accepted. The importance of feeling connected to my culture and family was immense. I missed my family and friends back home and the need for connection was growing like a ball of fire within me. I had no concept of my vulnerability concerning the need for community and a sense of belonging. This vulnerability made me unaware of the damage my mental health was suffering the longer I was a part of this church.

## Developing Religious Trauma

Religious trauma may happen from many different experiences inside or outside a church environment. It can come from messages that are persistently taught or the interactions that one has with the leader or people in authority. Religious trauma may also happen through family members or friends enforcing their beliefs onto their loved ones. In my case, my trauma included messages I received from my pastor.

My pastor was a charismatic leader. He possessed many positive qualities such as his humbleness, kindness, and empathy towards others. On the other hand, he was also a leader who attempted to motivate others by instilling shame, guilt, and fear. As I look back, much of what he spoke about was driven by the worry for others. And this worry for others was translated into motivating others to be the best they can be for God. His messages created perfectionism, which in turn fueled my anxiety to be the best I could be. When perfectionism is present, there is usually a belief that you are not good enough and that your mistakes, or in my case sins, are signs of personal flaws and that the only route to be truly accepted (in this case meaning being accepted by God) is to be perfect.

Fear was instilled through talking about needing to accept Jesus to get into the kingdom of heaven. Our pastor would suggest Hell may be a place for non-believers if God decides upon it, even if they are good people. I feared for my friends and colleagues at the time who were non-believers. Fear also surged through me as I learned demons were watching my every move.

My pastor made sure to tell the congregation that demons were watching us because they wanted us to fall into sin so they could take us to Hell with them. I grew paranoid because I knew I was not living up to God's standards for me. The paralyzing fear of going to Hell grew stronger every time I had premarital sex. This was considered a sin as well as masturbating, dishonesty, eating in excess, having sex with the same gender, and disobeying any commandment in the Bible.

Among other things we were suggested not to do, only celebrating Halloween in a particular way was included. We should only dress up as "holy" things, such as angels or other non-demonic beings. We should only worship God through traditional Christian music, not modern or "worldly" Christian music such as reggaeton or rap music. We were also taught not to trust our thoughts because our thoughts included three ways of thinking: our own thoughts, demon thoughts, and God's thoughts. We had to make sure we glorified God by listening to his thoughts and not listening to our own thoughts or "demon thoughts." Normal thoughts we all experience were seen as demonic thoughts trying to take control of our lives. This way of thinking teaches others to shut their thoughts and emotions down.

Pushing thoughts down goes against psychological practices we know are helpful today that teach acceptance. Acceptance allows us to not make meaning out of them because you can be at peace by letting them be just thoughts. The concept of acceptance in psychology means to non-judgmentally become aware of our thoughts and embrace our thoughts and feelings. Acceptance does not necessarily mean every single thought we have is true but more about not getting stuck in our thoughts and emotions regarding our experiences. Pushing down negative thoughts makes negative emotions harder to cope with because it teaches us to suppress them. Changing our mindset to a more positive and realistic way of thinking has also been shown to be helpful psychologically, but the issue is that we were taught to change or push down thoughts that are completely normal, such as wanting to listen to modern Christian music or wanting to dress up as a scary character for Halloween.

When we deny, minimize, and push down, we are invalidating our actual experiences instead of learning to work through and cope with our thoughts and emotions in a healthy way. Now, if you add the factor of trying to reach perfection to please God, you have yourself a rollercoaster of emotions. For me this included anxiety, depression, paranoia, and when things really took a turn for the worst, a psychotic breakdown.

My psychotic breakdown happened as a way to cope with the many things happening around me. I was feeling isolated as I was mostly focused on my schoolwork at the time. I stopped socializing and engaging in the activities that brought me joy mostly because of the amount of schoolwork I had. Even through these difficulties, my biggest stressor came from the anxiety and paranoia I developed within my church. During my psychotic episode, the auditory hallucinations became the voices of the demons I thought were talking to me and watching me closely. The voices were shaming me for having premarital sex. They were shaming me for all the things that I was taught were not "good" in God's eyes. They were telling me they were going to take me to Hell with them. I remember for a time in this psychotic state thinking I was already in Hell.

In my most vulnerable state, my pastor and his wife thought I must have done something sinful for having a psychotic episode. He and his wife asked me "What did you do?" and "Did you play with the Ouija board?" After multiple unsuccessful attempts at trying to figure out what my big sin must have been for experiencing psychosis, they went on to perform an exorcism. After hours of unsuccessful attempts at letting the demon out, the pastor looked at me and said, "Laura, stop, just stop already!" He did not know the impact these words and the exorcism had on feeding the shame, fear, helplessness, and powerlessness inside me. After feeling there was no hope for me, I called my family to take me back home.

Unfortunately, while I was back home, a few members of my family thought I had a demon in me and another exorcism was performed with a local Christian pastor. It was the same routine of trying to figure out what sinful thing I must have done to allow this demon to take over my mind. The pastor concluded that it was because I was having premarital sex and trying to speak in tongues, which was said to be God's language. According to him, I could not be sinning when I was speaking in God's language. SHAME! TERROR! GUILT! HELPLESS! WORTHLESS! BAD! SINNER! These were the true emotions and beliefs that were being intensified in my most vulnerable state, making my mental health worse.

Luckily, when praying the demon away evidently did not work, I requested my family take me to the hospital. I knew nothing else was working and my family and I needed to finally trust the professionals. Throughout the years after the exorcism, I was struggling with symptoms of post-traumatic stress and it was not until I saw a trauma therapist that I was finally able to fully heal from the trauma symptoms related to my religion. I finally received the help and medication I needed to get stable. If it was not for medication and therapy, I know my mental health would not have improved. It took me advocating for myself and allowing myself to trust the professionals and letting go of the belief that all I needed was prayer. The danger of some religious beliefs is the belief that people only need prayer for medical and mental health needs. Unfortunately, this is a damaging way of thinking because when people find it does not work for these needs, the person suffering suffers more.

They suffer more in believing they are damaged, helpless, and hopeless.

Mental health can suffer when we carry negative beliefs about ourselves and this is what believing exclusively in prayer does when thinking about medical and mental health. It sends the person the message that they have no hope, that they are helpless and they are the ones to blame because they are not getting better.

I can now say that I am happier and healthier. I have allowed myself to question my beliefs, to question the beliefs that were impacting my emotions in a negative manner. I've also allowed myself to redefine who God is for me. Knowing that I can let go of the God that influenced fear, shame, guilt, and helplessness inside me. I have healthily questioned my beliefs and come to the realization that I can let go of harmful beliefs and keep beliefs that instill positive emotions within me. These positive beliefs have allowed me to be the truest and most authentic version of myself I have ever been. It is my passion to work alongside other women who have felt their spiritual and/or religious beliefs have caused them harm or have not allowed them to become their truest authentic version of themselves. Authenticity is true freedom, and in freedom, there is more opportunity for peace and happiness.

**Tips for Women who are trying to Heal from Religious Trauma**

1. Find a community of people who understand you.

   A community that understands your struggles and who has also had their core beliefs questioned. Finding a community helps you feel less alone in your experience and more supported.

2. Identify and self-soothe.

   Identify what emotion you are experiencing, where you are experiencing it in your body, and choose a way to bring calm back into your mind and body. Try singing, humming, taking a hot bath, deep breathing, positive self-talk, journaling, yoga, or going on a walk.

3. Mindfulness.

   Mindfulness has been shown to have a positive impact on health and well-being. One of the ways to help you focus on the present experience is focusing on one of your five senses. Focus on smelling something soothing, listening to relaxing music, sipping a hot cup of tea, or feeling the warm water as you shower.

4. My personal favorite- Take back your power!

   Do something that you were taught not to do. Maybe you listen to a song you were told you should not listen to, say a few curse words, or like in my case, allow yourself to question your beliefs. Feeling empowered is key in healing from trauma.

5. Practice setting boundaries.

   Boundaries teach others how to treat you and send a message to yourself that you are to be respected. Start paying attention to how your boundaries are being pushed, ignored, or even shamed.

6. Find a therapist.

   Finding a therapist who understands the impacts of religious trauma is important for many people seeking to heal. Most people want to know their therapist understands them because of the therapist's experience with religion. For many, it is easier to feel connected when they know their therapist has a personal connection to what they are personally experiencing.

## Irene Karpadaki

Peace Health Enjoy
Psychologist, Coach & Founder

https://www.linkedin.com/in/irene-karpadaki-7b7064159
https://www.facebook.com/eirinh.karpadakh
https://www.instagram.com/irene_peace_health_enjoy/
https://peacehealthenjoy.systeme.io/

My name is Irene, in Greek - my mother tongue - it means Peace, and I have always been a Greatly Happy and Joyful being, enjoying helping people. I am a Psychologist, Coach, and Author with a M.Sc. in Psychology and Counseling from England, doing my research thesis on adults diagnosed with ADHD. I specialize in Global, Inclusive, Positive, Mindful, Soulful, and Heartful Teaching, Education, Pedagogy, Management, Coaching, Training, Parenting, and Leadership, and I have a B.A. in Education and Teaching. I completed my research thesis in Intercultural Education with refugees in Greece, I have researched, studied, and experienced the greatest systems and methodologies, not only theoretically, but have been traveling, working, studying, researching, and living in many different places. Globally, I am expanding my horizons, thirsty for growth and progress in places like the UK (the greatest when it comes to psychology research), Prague, and Finland (the greatest educational, organizational, and social systems globally), and right now am living in Paris, France where I founded Peace Health Enjoy!

# STORY BEHIND THE BRAND: PEACE HEALTH ENJOY

By Irene Karpadaki

Hi Glamorous Gorgeous Being!

My name is Irene, which in Greek, my mother tongue, means peace! Since my birth I have been Gifted with being always Happy, Joyful and have an enthusiastic high Glamorous Golden Glorious Energy just for…living! I have always loved helping others and transmitting positive energy. My grandmother was calling me *Hahanouliko* (coming from *haha*, meaning the girl who is always laughing!:D)

Through my relationships with other beings and my spiritual acknowledgment while growing up and traveling globally, seeing people struggling, suffering, living in anger, sadness, stress, depression, fear, scarcity, dissatisfaction or ungratefulness, I realized that gifts like these are rare. Through my studies in psychology, pedagogy, education, teaching, counseling, coaching, as well as working and teaching experience in management, organization and leadership, I learned the greatest strategies and ways to transmit that Gift of Peace, Health, and Joy and greatly helping people from all over the globe like you who is reading this. My goal is to help others earn Greater Happiness, Highest Glamorous Glorious Energy without needing cigarettes, sugar, energy drinks, or any other drugs, not even coffee, so you are improving your being organically, healthily to your greatest, highest potential!

Uncovering your Gorgeous, Genuine, Glamorous, Glorious, Gifted, Giving, Genius, Generous, Graceful, Grateful, Gold Gentle God and Goddess you are and living your Greatest Life, discovering infinite, highest valuable gems internally and externally! Helping people like you to uplift your spiritual, energetic, mental, emotional and physical health to be feeling, attracting, receiving, offering, experiencing, doing

GREAT, and going from just being to GORGEOUS GLORIOUS being.

My studies started at the age of seven, growing up in Crete, Greece, one of the most ancient civilizations alongside Egypt, reading great books and big novels that usually children are not choosing (e.g. Victor Hugo). This opened great horizons for me mentally so I started traveling as a teenager, firstly in Turkey with an exchange school program called *Building Bridges of Peace* between two countries that are taught in history school books that we are enemies (as all neighbor countries -schools are teaching ethnicism and wars- just one part of the history). But we created the greatest friendships, lifelong, loving, amazing relationships even though we spoke different languages. That was the first moment I learned that we are all a GLOBAL, Huge, Glamorous, Glorious Family and that no matter the different languages we speak, different cultures, lifestyles, or unique characteristics and fingerprints we have, the only thing that is connecting us ALL is our emotions. That is never changing no matter where you go on the globe; the way of expressing emotions differs but we are all having the same emotions! After that, I started traveling more and more, again in Turkey, studying education, pedagogy, English literature, photography, and arts in the Czech Republic for one year during my Bachelor's Degree in Education and Teaching in Greece, and living in a small town near Prague with people from literally all different continents, traveling, eating, celebrating, partying, studying, creating, living amazing experiences together, and learning from each other, exchanging and sharing our cultures and creating new, greater cultures together.

This is a part of my teachings; there is not only one shape. Just because it happened in the past and people started following it blindly, just because something is the "norm" does not mean it is right. For example, the idea that everything is a pyramid that we see in business coaching globally is so narrow minded; people are creating and you can be creating whatever shape you want! YOUR LIFE, YOUR DESIGN, YOUR PIECE OF ART! Of course we all belong and are part of this huge Glorious Glamorous Abundant Universal Family but each one of us has amazing, infinite, powerful strengths, unique talents and gifts - SUPER POWERS! And that is what I am helping people to find too and use for good.

I traveled, worked, and visited many places like the United Kingdom including England and Scotland, Germany, Spain, etc. and then I returned to Greece, doing my research thesis in Intercultural Education with refugees in Greece. I volunteered in Athens, helping families with young children, playing with them, teaching them, giving them clothes and necessary things, mediating between the Greek police, NGOs, and refugees to help them understand each other and help them live. The men refugees were thanking me, saying I was giving them the courage to continue living. That is the greatest reason why I am doing everything I do: helping, empowering, motivating, enlightening people to live a greater life with more Peace, Health, and Joy!

There I also learned -amongst plenty of other great lessons- after fainting from exhaustion because I was playing all day with kids, under the sun, giving all my energy without really caring for myself, the great importance of firstly giving yourself the care you need to be in a position of helping others too!

After finishing my studies in teaching and seeing the greatest problems in the globally anachronistic, old-school, traditional, outdated, education systems, I researched the greatest, most inclusive, modern educational- social - organizational systems globally (in Finland, living for one whole year there) and saw how amazing education can be, working in some of the greatest schools globally, moving to Paris, France where I worked in the greatest private Montessorian School in il de France. I finished my Master of Science in Psychology and

Counseling in England online, did my thesis research with adults having ADHD, and completed my internship stage at an association working with people with severe mental health diagnostics while working in the meantime in global companies in customer service, sales, management, teaching, and training with clients, colleagues, and more from all over the globe in all continents. I gained a global, vast knowledge of what is working, what is not working, why it is not working, and how it can be working GREATLY. I decided to offer all this knowledge through writing, coaching, counseling, mentoring and training online and in person globally!

Apart from the science and academics, I have been of course going through my own healing journey, from being overweight and living as a child in an overweight, Christian Orthodox Greek family (considerably, gratefully more open minded than others, thank GOD but still), to right now having a great, strong, healthy, sexy body that is admired, loved, respected, and greatly cared for firstly by myself. I overcame many obstacles and went through Hell to get to Heaven where I am living right now (in Paris, France). I am forever studying spirituality and well-being. I offer complete coaching, going from well-being to GORGEOUS-Being training and educational, pedagogical, teaching, parenting, global management, and leadership training regarding all areas of peace, health, and joy! Also I am teaching you to create GREAT change and improvement in all the Golden 5 areas of your being which are:

1. Physical - everything you experience through your senses in the pragmatic world.

2. Emotional - feelings, emotional intelligence, and regulation. Emotional intelligence is one of the most underrated, most powerful, strong skills; use it to create good magic for you and others!

3. Energetic- vibration cleansing energy is as highly needed as

cleaning your physical body because if not, it blocks your greatest gifts and abundance of peace, health, joy, love, pleasure, happiness, money, great beings, great offers, relationships, satisfaction, and great experiences from coming into your physical world - the pragmatic reality! I show you how to be cleansing, enlightening, uplifting, directing, growing, glowing, and use energy for doing GREAT, receiving, and offering glamour!Golden Loving Energy, the most powerful, healing, enlightening, uplifting, encouraging, positively transformational energy!

4. Mental - your thoughts; mindset! Thoughts create energy, which influences your emotions and creates the physical, pragmatic reality you live in. I am going to teach you how to create the Greatest, most Glorious, Genuine, Genius, Glamorous, Golden, confident, strong, powerful, happy, beautiful mindset so you are creating a happy, glorious, amazingly beautiful, fulfilling life!

5. Spiritual- your Highest, Greatest, Glorious, Genuine, Gold, your God and Goddess, your gut, and your genius self that is all knowing. It is enlightening and uplifting when learning how to access it, heal it, love it, and trust it and that's what we are doing together!

All these are highly needed no matter your level right now or personal-professional situation, helping you leverage up and uplift you even GREATER in all those areas of your gorgeous being so that you are reaching even greater, deeper levels of self-acknowledgment, positive change and healing, and being more peaceful, healthy, and joyful in all areas of your life!

All these areas, parenting, teaching, coaching, counseling, mentoring, management, and leadership are connected. I'm showing you how and helping you be GREATER in all ways for you and the global GOOD!

This is your calling to GO HIGHER!

I am inviting you to contact me and let's GROW and GLOW! Global changes are happening. Through my coaching you are going to for sure create greater changes with more Peace, Health, and en…JOY!

**REMEMBER:**
**YOU ARE NOT JUST A DROP IN THE OCEAN…**

## Lourdes Auquilla

Lourdes Auquilla, LLC
Latina Bookkeeper

https://www.linkedin.com/in/lourdes-auquilla-526696190/
https://www.facebook.com/lourdesauquillabookkeeping
https://www.instagram.com/lourdesbookss/
https://www.lourdesauquilla.com/
https://www.lourdesauquilla.com/quote

Lourdes was raised by Ecuadorian parents in NYC. She's always admired their hustle, so she became a hustler herself. She started her entrepreneur story when she was 16 by selling spider plants in her school. After starting many small businesses, she realized that the reason why she was so passionate about business was because when she knew her numbers, she realized she could make more money and live her dream life. She wanted to help other business owners do the same. She went to Monroe College and graduated with a BBA in Accounting. She managed to skip corporate and took courses that taught her the skills to become a bookkeeper. Today, she is a 21-year-old Latina Bookkeeper who has helped over 20 business owners with their bookkeeping by showing them exactly where their hard-earned money is going, helping them be tax-ready, and growing their profits!

# BREAKING GENERATIONAL CHAINS

By Lourdes Auquilla

I was born and raised in New York City. My parents came from Ecuador, and seeing the way they hustled their way to NYC was very inspiring for me. I had seen the obstacles my parents had to face as immigrants, like not being able to get a high-paying job because of their status, and being taken advantage of financially by their employers. I felt that as a daughter of immigrants, it was my job to give back to my parents by doing something amazing in my life that would ensure financial stability for my parents and myself. That's a huge responsibility to have on you as a young child.

Being the unique person that I was, I did the exact opposite of what my parents did, and started a business instead of going to the typical and "secure" 9-5 job my family chose. It's tough because when you're the first in your family to do this, you're breaking generational chains that have been put on you against your will, and it's up to you to break through them, stop the patterns, and introduce new ones.

My first entrepreneurial venture started in John Bowne High School. One of my teachers had a lot of spare spider plants, and asked who wanted them. I impulsively raised my hand even though I barely had space for them at home. Time passed, and my plants grew... a lot. I didn't know where to keep them, so I decided to sell them. My dad brought me pots. My dear friends, family, and neighbors purchased them. I ended up making at least $200 off the plants. I grew fond of the business world because of this.

Choosing the entrepreneurial path as an introvert was not an ideal choice, as you can imagine. Having to put yourself out there is something crazy - especially when your audience is a bunch of high school students. Then came my second attempt at business: selling sandwiches at John Bowne High School. If you're from NYC, you know the bacon egg and cheese sandwich is our national food, along with a beverage like an Arizona. Don't get caught without one, or else someone will yell out "NO BEV!"

I would wake up every Monday, Wednesday, and Friday at 5am to make these sandwiches and pack them up in a cooler bag. I expanded to selling drinks as well for the perfect meal combo. You can imagine the hassle it was to bring two big cooler bags into a high school and pass them through metal detectors most mornings.

I would walk around the cafeteria asking if anyone wanted to have some. I got some weird looks, mean comments, and laughed at, but I also got some excitement and people would crowd me in the cafeteria to buy some sandwiches. Eventually, I would have random people approach me for my sandwiches. I don't mean to brag, but my sandwiches were fire, and affordable. You got a whole meal for $5! I eventually sold Icees but that wasn't successful. I remember one time, I sold a slightly melted one to some kid, and he told me about it the next day. I gave him one or two for free. He became a loyal client after. If I can tell you some lessons about business from this experience, it's that it's better to lose a dollar than a customer.

There was a point where someone stole my earnings for the day ($80). I was pissed. However, remember that when you're in business, your growth won't be linear all the time. There are times when you'll be down, but life works in waves, and what is down, must come up. So never lose hope and remain resilient because there is an abundance of wealth on the other side. You just have to keep going.

I found that abundance of wealth in my current bookkeeping business. Being wealthy means something different to everyone. You have to figure out what wealth means to you. Then, your business can be built to support that dream.

I vividly remember speaking to an old friend of mine in the high school cafeteria about what we'd do after graduating. I told him I wanted to open a business, but not in accounting because it's so "plain and boring". Oh, the irony.

My online business venture started when I was in my first semester of college. I was curious and searched for businesses to do from home. I met a coach, Paige, who offered to coach me, and I would help with her Instagram engagement. I agreed and realized it wasn't for me. Then, she introduced me to bookkeeping. I looked into it, and it was a match made in heaven. She was the first coach I ever had and paved my way to success. I was already in college pursuing my BBA in Accounting, so why not?

Time passed, and I dove into bookkeeping. I joined a Facebook group, where I first heard about my current bookkeeping coach, Katie Ferro, CPA. She invited me to join a group of bookkeepers, and I felt welcomed. I remember she posted about her program Become a Bookkeeper. I purchased the payment plan & was in.

However, a lot of people did not see my vision. My mom at first, would not tell her friends I had a business, and wouldn't share my excitement of my wins. It made me feel really crappy because to me her validation is everything. My dad was hesitant to help me invest in Katie's second program because he thought it was not the best move for me. I was really stressed and did Shipt at that time and other side hustles, so I started thinking about the hours I would have to put in to afford the program. I even considered taking out a loan to afford this. I felt hopeless. I remember telling my best friend Kelly about it, and just crying in the bathroom.

A week later, my dad changed his mind and told me he'd pay for the program but to do it fast before he changed his mind. You know how Hispanic parents are. That opened the door to success for me.

Through trial and error, I landed my first dream client. The work was not dreamy, but Katie made it doable. I spent more than 24 hours on it. Based on that experience, and many other experiences, I'd like to share some bookkeeping tips that will help you avoid going through the struggles my previous clients had gone through to save you the stress:

1. Open a separate business checking account. Don't combine business and personal funds, because if you have an LLC, you risk losing the protection it provides. Also, commingling makes bookkeeping and tax time harder because then you're spending more time figuring out if an expense is personal or business. Plus, you risk missing out on tax deductions if you co-mingle funds.

2. Do your monthly bookkeeping. When you know what's going on with your money on a monthly basis, you're able to adjust your offers by raising prices, cutting expenses, or getting more clients. You're also able to cut or adjust any expenses throughout the year versus looking at reports at year-end and regretting investing in a course you didn't even take full advantage of.

3. Set 15-30% of your profits for taxes in a separate bank account. When you do this monthly, you'll have money set aside for the tax bill instead of getting that tax bill shock when filing taxes.

4. If you're struggling to keep up with your bookkeeping or you just don't know what the heck you're doing, hire me!

Fast forward to today; I am running a successful, scalable, and profitable bookkeeping business, and most of my client work takes less than an hour to complete. My mom brags to everyone about my business, and my dad is proud of me. Katie always reminds me that I am living the life I dreamt of. I have been able to invest in a money coach, Debbie, who has really helped transform my entire life because, like she says, "money touches everything", and when your finances are in order, everything else flows.

You need to surround yourself with people who will celebrate your wins and believe in collaboration, not competition. Don't be afraid to speak to "strangers" in business. They might end up being one of your biggest supporters, like Jennifer, who I appreciate for giving me the opportunity to be a part of this book.

Today, I have helped more than 20 business owners who are tired of not knowing where their hard-earned money is going, and who want to be tax-ready and grow their profits.

The hustle was worth it, because life gets to be simple now, and I get to help business owners feel the same way when they know where their money is going, which ultimately results in living their dream life.

## Irisneri Alicea

Founder of Descubre Tu Historia

https://www.linkedin.com/in/irisneri-alicea-flores-75a7477/
https://www.facebook.com/descubretuhistoria21
https://www.instagram.com/descubretuhistoria/
https://www.descubretuhistoria.com/

Latina Professional Genealogist Irisneri Alicea Flores decided four years ago to pursue her dreams of helping Latinos/Latinas through the empowering and healing journey of Genealogy. She sees Genealogy as one of the gateways to connect to our roots, our ancestors, and our ancestral countries. By looking at our ancestors' stories more closely, we can understand better the whys. It can also inspire the tough conversations that for so long fell under "de eso no se habla". It can help someone who has longed to connect to their ancestral culture and country to finally feel that connection. Inspired by how needed this important piece was within our community, four years ago she founded Descubre Tu Historia. Today, she lives out her dream of helping people connect to their roots and guide them through the empowering and healing journey. She is also a speaker who helps Latinos by providing information on how to start, resources readily available, and genealogy tips and insights on Spanish documents.

# THE MAGIC OF NOSOTRAS

By Irisneri Alicea

In the fabric of life, sometimes the most profound transformations are woven from threads of doubt and uncertainty. Four years ago I opened my heart to a group of women and discovered what happens when we support, uplift, and trust each other.

While my journey to finding my passion and what I loved started 11 years ago, I did not dare to act on it until four years ago. Why did I not act on it? Let me list the reasons...

"I don't have the proper credentials."

"I am almost 40 years old, it is just too late."

"After working in Human Resources for almost 20 years, how can I just quit?"

"It is irresponsible of me to just start a new career; what about my kids and husband?"

"What will my family say?"

"It would be too selfish of me."

Sound familiar? Yes I know, some of these you probably say to yourself. So let me just say this to you, because understanding, embracing, and accepting this was instrumental for me and that is, "you are not alone".

On October 18, 2018, I sat with a group of people at my former job, which was huge because for the first time, I allowed myself to say yes and be a part of something. We sat and watched a documentary called "Project Enye" by Denise Soler Cox. I watched and listened to Denise talk about the experiences of first-generation Latinos growing up between two cultures and its effects on all of us. For the first time in my life someone was putting words to my experiences and that, no, I had not imagined these feelings nor was I being too "sensitive". As my colleagues sat there, nodding their heads vigorously in recognition or with tears in their eyes, we all collectively felt the same thing - we were not alone. It was truly one of the first times that I stood with a group of people and opened up and talked about what each of us had experienced growing up. I spoke about things I had never felt safe talking to anyone about. As I very reluctantly left the room because I just did not want to stop the conversation, I left with a goal, and that was that I needed to meet this person some way, somehow. She was a Latina who not only spoke the truth about deep-rooted feelings, but she also was someone who had a dream of doing this documentary, despite not going to film school. 17 years went by from the night this idea was born and one day she decided to go for it and she did it! Now she is a filmmaker, sought-after speaker, and inspiring many of us to think about our dreams and helping us make our dreams come true. So I wrote an email to see if she would come to speak for an event in the Spring of 2019. *This is where I chose to trust my instincts and did something despite the fear I felt.* What if they did not get back to me? But guess what? She did!

April of 2019 was here and with major nerves taking over, I was just moments away from meeting the person that my instincts said I needed to meet. Because she woke up the Iris that had been dormant for so long, the dreamer, the go-getter, the one that if she wanted it bad enough could make it happen. The Iris that my mom struggled for me to see again, but life had happened, and I was blinded by the blows and fears that had come my way. The Iris that was so far removed from me that felt like a completely different person, did she ever exist?

My colleagues, understanding what an important moment it was for me to meet Denise, arranged for me to escort her to where she was to speak. As we walked into the elevator my heart was pounding because

I truly felt it was now or never. After months of reading her posts about finding our purpose, the other Iris that I had thought no longer was a part of me took over and blurted out her dream. "My dream is to be a genealogist and help Latinos find and connect to their roots, help them heal through the information they can find, and empower them with what they can learn, because it is important for us to know where we come from." She looked at me with a big smile on her face, eyes glowing with excitement and she said "Mujer, you have to do it, we are going to talk later, I love it!" At that point my mouth dropped to the floor, panic set in, and I said in my head, "Iris, what did you do??!" I don't think I stopped shaking the whole day!

Later that night I was her ride from dinner to her hotel. Once we got into my car I could not believe it when she started to ask me questions, and an hour and a half later we were still talking about my dreams! I dropped her off really feeling like I could make this happen! She saw me, she heard me, and she got it because she was that Latina who also fought against her own internal dialogue, but despite all that she made her dream of creating a documentary come true. We agreed she would reach out again because she would love to work with me. I went home knowing life was never going to be the same. But with time, panic set in yet again and the old internal dialogue started again. A few months later when I heard from her asking me to join her program to help Latinas like me make their dreams come true, I had almost convinced myself "I can't do this," and I used all the excuses, time, finances…I actually said no.

The last day of registration was here and I was still saying no. I spoke to my little sister, and after hearing all my "reasons" as to why I could not do it now, we ended our conversation - or so I thought. Later that day, very close to the last hour before registration was to close, she called me and said, "I just sent you the money sister; this is your time, it is time. You have to do this for yourself, say yes to yourself." I was shocked, and my heart and brain wanted to burst, but all my arguments went out the window and I accepted the help. I made her a promise that I would do this. I promised her I would put my all into it and for the first time in a long time, I said yes to myself. Then my kids came into my mind and I thought about how I have always told them, "Do what you love and what makes you happy." This was my moment to show them it was possible.

I entered the program with no idea of what to expect, but it was the beginning of the most magical journey. While all the fears were present, for the first time they took a back seat and I did not let them stop me. I went in with an open heart and mind, allowing myself to be vulnerable with people I barely knew at the time. I allowed myself to be challenged in a way I never had before and trusted. I was surrounded by Mujeres that I would quietly look at the screen during our meetings and be in complete awe not believing that I was among authors, entrepreneurs, and activists who were all doing or hoping to do what they have always dreamed of. The same excitement Denise had shown me about my dream they did too. We all shared our struggles, from business to personal. Slowly many of us started to form bonds and started to collaborate. This is when I learned about the magic that occurs when you surround yourself with women who uplift and empower each other. Many of these women came in with ideas and desires and like me battled against internal dialogues set in by society and our cultures. But we all saw each other and truly believed in what we wanted to do. As time went on we watched as each of us started to become what we always dreamed.

On July 31, 2019, I founded Descubre Tu Historia and accepted my first investigation as a professional genealogist, only two months after starting the program. By finally trusting myself, saying yes to myself, accepting help, and opening my heart to others, I reconnected to my core self. I unburied the speaker in me, and now I hold speaking events about genealogy and helping Latinos do their own research. Making them aware of the resources that are available to us, teaching our community that while we are not in many history books, our "gente" was there. After two years I left my full-time job and now I live my dream of every day helping Latinos uncover their family history. I help our community realize that genealogy is one of the doors to help them connect to their roots and their ancestral countries. That when we uncover the past, while some of the truths are difficult to process, this is where the healing occurs for many of us; not by burying it and not talking about it.

But none of this would have happened without my Mom who always stands by me, without my sister and my daughter, who are my forever cheerleaders. And without the Mujeres that now, four years later, I call my friends and family, that without the magic of nosotras I would not be here doing what I love. As a true historian and genealogist I hereby document my forever, thank you to all of you.

So how can you start your own journey? Remember these lessons:

- Start trusting yourself and listening to your instincts.
- Say yes to yourself.
- Start doing things despite the fear, especially when you imagine yourself doing that thing and it fills you with excitement.
- Learn to give yourself grace, we are human after all.
- Imperfect action.
- Accept help.
- Surround yourself with "Mujeres" that will empower you and lovingly and firmly challenge you.
- Glow in the magic that occurs.

## Jacklyn Collins

JC Business Coaching
Business Coach

https://www.facebook.com/profile.php?id=100090307331520&mibextid=9R9pXO
https://www.instagram.com/thejacklynhopkins/
https://www.facebook.com/groups/creativefemaleentrepreneurs1

Jacklyn Collins, born and raised in Toronto, Canada, is on a mission to empower female coaches and entrepreneurs. Her core focus centers on creating vibrant communities that boost their visibility so they can get more clients. Jacklyn brings to the table a rich blend of skills as a certified coach and a full-time marketing consultant, underpinned by her background in the corporate world. What sets Jacklyn apart is her innate creativity and her ability to infuse it into her work. She's a true creative at heart, and when she's not busy helping her clients succeed, she's immersing herself in the beauty of nature and drawing inspiration from its tranquility. Jacklyn's dedication to her clients and unwavering passion for both coaching and entrepreneurship make her a standout figure in her field. She believes that by building engaged communities and harnessing the power of visibility, women can unlock their full potential and achieve remarkable success.

# BREAKING FREE

By Jacklyn Collins

## Early Roots and Inspirational Beginnings

My personal journey is deeply rooted in my upbringing. From my earliest days, I had always felt like an outsider. Picture this: an eight-year-old girl in bell-bottom jeans that I had long since outgrown, the hem brushing just above my ankles. "Your jeans don't fit you" and "You're so shy" were some of the most frequent statements I heard, becoming a familiar echo. Forming friendships was a challenge as I struggled with the complexities of social interaction, seeking connection without embracing the label of "different". A subtle undertone of not quite fitting in was starting to take over, a feeling that people might not truly resonate with me. Unbeknownst to me, the dynamics of my home life were influencing and shaping my behavior, spilling over to my teenage years and eventually, adulthood.

My parents had just gotten divorced. All I truly understood at that time was that Mommy and Daddy were no longer living together. The routine settled in—Dad's Thursdays were a bi-weekly thing, and in between, it was weekend visits. Amidst the chaos, my mind held onto intense arguments. Even today, I can still recall hiding beneath the dining table because it felt like my safest haven.

With this divorce, the script of our lives underwent a rewrite. My mom, newly single, took on the weight of her business alongside the financial responsibility for herself, my brother, and yours truly.

I started to witness my mother's unwavering determination as a single parent and entrepreneur. Her entrepreneurial struggles and successes became the foundation of my own aspirations. The unbreakable determination with which she navigated the challenges of business ownership left a lasting mark on my spirit, preparing me for the road ahead and the challenges that would ultimately shape my journey.

## Surviving the Messy Lessons of My Twenties

During my teenage years, I landed my first-ever job as a cashier. I recall getting home from work after a shift and telling my mom, "That felt like the longest day ever!" In truth, it genuinely stretched on, but there was something empowering about it. I was earning my own money for the first time, finally capable of covering my own phone bill. It's astonishing how $10 back then feels like $1000 today.

High school graduation was on the horizon, accompanied by the pressure to have a concrete plan for post-secondary life. The reality? I had absolutely no clue what I wanted to do with my life. The notion of having my life's purpose all figured out at eighteen was a far-fetched concept to me. I wondered, *How do people just know*? I sent a few applications to universities, securing acceptance to one, only to defer my offer so that I could continue working part-time and ultimately save up enough money to support my post-secondary endeavors.

Eventually, I veered towards college. The candid truth was that university seemed financially unattainable, and an inkling emerged that it wasn't my destined path. I chose to study Fashion Management, which eventually led me to earn a college diploma within a span of two years.

Entering my early twenties post-college, I landed a full-time gig at a headquarters for a well-known clothing brand. College had painted a utopian picture of the 9-to-5 lifestyle with financial prosperity. Reality, however, hit me hard. The office higher-ups weren't exactly champions of my success, and a 9-hour workday meant a $35,000 annual salary. Just before my probationary term was over, they terminated my employment, revealing later that they never intended to hire someone permanently. It was time for a change, so I transitioned to a different company with a period of contract employment. My trajectory propelled me to full-time status and within six months, I secured a promotion. Optimism finally emerged. That is, until it abruptly dimmed. A year later, the company went under, leaving me jobless once more.

These are only a couple of snapshots from my experiences in my twenties in the realm of full-time jobs. Job changes became the norm, resulting in four firings due to circumstances beyond my control.

It wasn't until my late twenties that I started looking deep within. I came to understand that job security is an illusion, and my pursuit of full-time positions was a quest for emotional and financial stability. Consequently, I found myself in jobs that guaranteed financial security but lacked personal fulfillment. Through this committed journey of self-discovery and personal growth, I also recognized that life is too short for mediocrity. This awareness motivated me to view life differently and sparked a significant shift in my path. Rather than sacrificing my dreams for financial stability, I started to actively pursue long-term aspirations.

## Current Endeavours

As I began to appreciate my self-worth and value as an individual, I secured a position in marketing that aligned with my goals and overall visions. In addition, I'm an entrepreneur on the side, assisting fellow business owners in establishing engaged communities using Facebook to attract clients.

Throughout my journey, experiences, observations, and insights, I learned to acknowledge the transformative power of community. The advantages of having an engaged audience are twofold: it creates a platform for a supportive network and unlocks boundless possibilities for sales. Even the most determined entrepreneurs, including my own mother, encountered moments of uncertainty stemming from a shortage of clients. The absence of a nurturing and uplifting network could pose significant barriers to attaining growth and prosperity.

## Tips for Success

Navigating the complexities of life's journey is a process marked by diverse experiences, unforeseen challenges, and transformative growth. From the roots of my early upbringing to the trials and triumphs of my twenties, my personal odyssey has been an evolving story of self-discovery, perseverance, and resilience. Drawing inspiration from my own path, I've gathered valuable insights and tips that can guide and empower others in their pursuit of success and fulfillment. These lessons, gathered from the unique blend of my past, emphasize the significance of embracing individuality, seeking authenticity, and leveraging personal strengths. Through this narrative, I invite you to explore tips of wisdom that can illuminate your way forward.

Embrace Individuality: Just as my unique upbringing shaped my journey, recognize that your personal story is your strength. Embrace your individuality and use it to build your distinct identity in your chosen field.

Seek Authenticity: Explore your passions and values. Pursue endeavors that resonate with your true self, as they will provide lasting fulfillment on your journey.

Embrace Change: Don't fear change or uncertainty. Instead, use them as stepping stones towards growth. Embrace new opportunities and be open to adjusting your path as needed.

Leverage Your Creativity: Creativity is a valuable asset for problem-solving and innovation. Use your unique perspective to develop innovative solutions.

Prioritise Personal Development: Invest in yourself through continuous learning and personal growth. Strengthen your skills and mindset to overcome challenges and seize opportunities.

Set Clear Goals: Define your goals with clarity and purpose. Break them down into actionable steps to maintain focus and motivation.

Build a Supportive Network: A supportive community is essential for success. Surround yourself with mentors, peers, and fellow entrepreneurs or others in your field who uplift and inspire you.

Celebrate Progress and Successes: Acknowledge and celebrate your milestones, no matter how small. Recognize that your achievements can boost your confidence and propel you forward.

Incorporating these principles into your journey will empower you to navigate the complexities of life and work, building a path that aligns with your passions and aspirations.

## Final Thoughts

Just as I navigated numerous challenges and forged my own path, you too can harness these lessons to steer your journey towards success.

Remember, embracing your individuality and seeking authentic purpose are essential components of your entrepreneurial voyage. Don't shy away from change or setbacks; rather, view them as valuable learning opportunities that shape your growth.

As you chart your course, prioritize your personal development, set clear goals, and dare to dream big. The realization that life is too short for mediocrity is a driving force that can push you beyond your comfort zone. Embrace this awareness, view challenges as stepping stones, and actively pursue your aspirations with determination and resilience.

In the end, your journey is uniquely yours, just as mine has been mine. By absorbing these lessons, you gain the tools to forge ahead, transform challenges into triumphs, and create a lasting impact in your chosen path. The path to success is a winding one, but with the right mindset, community, and dedication, you can overcome any obstacle and leave your mark on the world. Your journey starts now; empower yourself, pursue your passions, and create the legacy you envision.

## **Cynthia Puga**

NBC/ Telemundo
Journalist

www.linkedin.com/in/cynthia-puga-3b141b189
https://www.facebook.com/profile.php?id=100010294923517
www.instagram.com/cynthiapugatv

Cynthia Puga is a journalist and writer currently living in the state of Washington. She was born and raised in Oxnard, California, and studied at California State University, Northridge where she received her Bachelor's Degree in Broadcast Journalism. She enjoys telling the stories of others and spending time with her friends and family.

# ADMIRING THE THORN OF A ROSE

## By Cynthia Puga

When you're a kid, there seem to be no worries in the world, yet you have that feeling or need to grow up quickly. Now, fast forward to adulthood where you're no longer playing with your school friends and you're taking phone calls in an office while trying to stay awake, sipping on a cup of coffee from work that does not taste like that dream of being older.

While I was growing up, I realized that some kids had to grow up quicker than others. I am a daughter of immigrant parents and from a young age, I learned to become a translator and fill out paperwork. I also tried to work harder than anyone else in the room. Why is that? Because my parents wanted the best for me and I felt the pressure of giving back to them.

So, you begin to place this great pressure on yourself that you have to follow a specific path to be "successful" when in fact, there is no right or wrong path. I've learned that every single individual has their own journey and experiences they will go through in life. I thought my path was to become a radiologist and be a successful worker in the medical field. Let me tell you this: I hated math and science. Not only were my grades suffering, but my mental health was also being affected.

I decided to take a break from university after the second year to figure out what I wanted for myself, not what the "Perfect Daughter" wanted.

My mother was furious.

She continued to tell me I wouldn't finish school if I took a break and that I had to at least get to the finish line. Yet, how was I supposed to graduate when I was going in circles with my own thoughts and choices?

A rose grows thorns in order to survive. I had to learn how to admire the thorn on a rose, the scars that would eventually grow to protect me and make me stronger. Each prick is a reminder of the challenges we've had to face in life. I had to learn how to put my foot down, make my own path, and decide what I wanted for myself. Not follow what society considers "correct." People may think your life is as perfect as a rose, but what they don't see are the roots and the thorns you had to grow to show off the beautiful yet delicate petals that they see now.

My parents eventually came around and began to realize this was my life to follow. I've been fortunate enough to have them both by my side giving me advice along the way, not only as parents but as friends.

During my year-long break from school, I began to research different career paths. I always had an infatuation with writing, so I thought about majoring in English, but wasn't sure what I'd do with that. The next major I looked into was journalism, but I also couldn't picture myself in the field. I declared it as my major anyway. At that moment, my mindset was, "It doesn't hurt to try something completely new," even though it terrified me.

As the new school year began, I was still struggling with my mental health while attending classes. To make matters worse, I quickly realized it was my job to talk to people and strangers in the journalism world.

I went into sheer panic. I was never a social butterfly as a kid and never learned how to hold a conversation. What was I thinking? Why would I jump into something I was not comfortable doing?

That sentence.

That exact sentence is the reason life has taken me through some of the best experiences in my life.

If you begin to back off from something you've been wanting to do, do it anyway. No matter how much fear and adrenaline begin to run through your head. Once you do it, you'll begin to question why you hadn't done it earlier.

Learning this has opened multiple doors for me in many different industries. Overcoming that fear of being in a new setting has become the new normal and it definitely was not easy to get there.

Since then, I've been a background actress on sets of shows like *Euphoria*, *Jane the Virgin*, *Minx*, and so many others. I became a published author for my university after submitting an essay along with a few other students that would inspire the incoming freshmen going into their first English class. I am now a journalist working in the state of Washington for an NBC affiliate news station. I am also an anchor, producer, and writer for Telemundo at that same station.

After getting a taste of what it was like working on set, I fell in love with production. Whether I was in front of the camera as a talent or behind the scenes, it felt right. And that's when I realized I found my calling.

There was a spark in my chest that was telling me I was meant to do this. I was meant to tell stories.

Removing the doubt in our heads is easier said than done, but I decided to create a journey that I would be content with. That comes with a lot of uncomfortable sacrifices.

I moved over 1,000 miles away from my family to a completely new state to begin a new job I still wasn't sure I was fit for.

I became a news anchor and producer after having been a morning news reporter for about 5 months. As journalists, the majority of us begin at smaller stations, but what they don't tell you is that you'll be taking on multiple roles at once while receiving the bare minimum wage. I'm what you'd call a "one-woman show" in this position. To give you an inside scoop: I produce our news rundown, meaning I write the stories that will be on our newscast, I do the weather, write articles for the website, manage the social media accounts, and anchor the newscast.

You would think, having a career straight out of college would mean being fulfilled with no worries in the world. But after two months of being away from home, I wanted to quit.

I wanted to return to the place I felt comfortable in. My parents told me I couldn't go back home; I had to finish my two-year contract first at this job.

At that moment, it felt like the world was shattering. I cut contact with every person I knew for a month because, in my mind, no one was supporting my decisions. I had to learn to manage being uncomfortable in situations where no one could physically be there for me and be okay with feeling every emotion in that moment.

To this day I'm grateful they let me struggle on my own. I had to find a place where I felt grounded. I got to know myself a million times more than I would have if I hadn't taken the risk and the job offer.

Every prick and scar gave me the strength to bloom into the person I am today.

You soon come to realize that the thorn is what helps a rose survive. The experiences you learn to endure, help your self-confidence unfold throughout time.

Sometimes I wish I could hug the younger version of myself and tell her it's all going to turn out okay. Don't let society pressure you into thinking you should be living one way when you're capable of doing much more than that. You only go as far as you allow yourself to.

So don't limit yourself.

## Sandra Nuñez

Founder of Educated Chingona

www.linkedin.com/in/sandra-nunez-32534875
https://www.instagram.com/educatedchingona/

My name is Sandra Nunez and I am a first-gen Mexicana. I am part of the 3% of former foster youths who made it to college. I am proud of my journey and the many doors it has opened for me, but even more proud of the doors I opened by sharing my story. Coming from a world where education was never talked about, I am blessed that I have been able to continue my journey. I changed the narrative for my family, and that's a big deal. My passion is spreading empowerment. Many will say education is a waste, but many more will say it has helped them flourish into cycle breakers. We are contributing to the much-needed representation in academia. See, we're not just doing it for us; we do it for those who don't feel "they have what it takes" or "like they don't belong". You belong, we all belong.

# MY CHINGONA ERA: A JOURNEY OF RESILIENCE AND SELF-DISCOVERY

By Sandra Nuñez

My story is one of triumphs and breaking barriers, one that is consistently being worked on, a story of statistics and an unfortunate deck of life cards. I feel like my life has consistently been under construction and, not to say there's anything wrong with that, but stability and calmness are what I have always yearned for. We all know that construction sites definitely don't provide stability or calmness, but here I am. Here I am thriving in the world that was created to make me feel like I do not belong. Statistics said I would never make it this far. Doubters believed that I wouldn't be successful, and those who have hurt me in life thought they would destroy me. I've been raped, abandoned, told that I'm not lovable, beaten, and mentally, emotionally, and physically abused. I experienced life within the Foster system and became a teen mom at the age of 13. I learned to cope and numb myself with alcohol and pill usage. So what I want you to take away from this chapter is *hope* - it's never too late to find yourself. It's never too late to find your voice, it's never too late to begin to believe in yourself. Remember healing is possible, happiness is an option and please, please always remember you are not alone.

My name is Sandra Nuñez. I am a proud Mexican-American woman who was born and raised in Escondido, CA. I am 36 years young and have four children who I live for daily. I have been through hell and back and decided years ago that I would never allow what I have been through to stop me from becoming my best self. I am a proud first-generation college student who defied all odds! I am proud of my educational journey. I am proud to share my story. Those who know me know if it involves college/education, I AM YOUR GIRL! It is an honor to be known as that person. It makes my heart so happy to see women pursuing higher education because I have seen how many doors of opportunity it has opened for me. I have been able to thrive and blossom in these spaces. And the reasons mentioned above are exactly why I began my business, my platform, and my beautiful community, that I call *Chingonahood*. I feel like in a world of constantly needing to do more, finding ways to succeed, and finding ways to do better in life, all while juggling motherhood, work, relationships, and self-care, we lose sight of other things that are important. Like our sanity. Sometimes, in this busy world we live in, we get so caught up in trying to take care of everyone around us that we abandon our own needs. So, I wanted to create a platform that many women could relate to and find community in. And that's exactly what I have been to create. I am not alone in this world. Many thousands out there have also lived through the struggles, hardships, obstacles, and life experiences that I have endured. Those stories give me hope.

Along our educational journeys, we need fuel, we need encouragement, and we need to believe in ourselves. So I became that person for myself when I needed it the most. Sometimes we need tough love and honesty, not a "beat around the bush pep talk", and sometimes we need to know that we are not alone. There are many of us out here trying to figure life out, trying to make something of ourselves, trying to create spaces where we feel seen and feel like we belong. Then I thought, why not share it with the world? Why not share it with other Chingonas who need a pick-me-up? What if there are more people like me out there? I decided to create this platform, Educated Chingona, in which I share my words, whether they're words of encouragement or reflections - and look at where we are now!

I needed to find a community of women who were pursuing higher education while also parenting and trying to find a balance in life. Because as hard as it was, I knew there were others out there getting it done, and I needed to find people who understood the struggle and didn't try to persuade me to quit just because things got hard.

Managing this platform has definitely not been easy. It made me question so much and second-guess everything I do and how I navigate the platform. There have been multiple times over the years that I've almost completely just stopped doing it. Because I asked myself, "Who the heck would want to listen to me and what I have to say?" I created my platform back in 2019 and here we are today with almost 22,000 supporters. I just want to highlight that this did not happen overnight. It took years to get to where I am today. It took a lot of vulnerability, transparency, and fighting my own demons. In order to be authentic on this platform, I needed to come to terms with a lot of things that have happened in my life. There's definitely a lot of reflection that goes on with what I post. Everything that I post is intentional and never scheduled or pre-planned unless it is a holiday. I try to give 1000% of who I truly am and what it is that I'm going through in life. I am not ashamed of my past, nor am I ashamed of what I have experienced.

I find that my platform is different in that it is a safe space, and not just a safe space but a very vulnerable one. Despite this, I feel quite comfortable bearing my life story in hopes that it reaches the person who needs to hear it most and instills that hope, faith, and light that we all need in life when we are feeling alone and like there's no other way out. Feeling like life will never get easier. I want to highlight that even through the messiness of life, things do get better. The healing journey is rough. But who better than to do it than you? Why not you? It's always been you. We just have to learn to believe in ourselves a little stronger. I share so many aspects of my life, these aspects that complete the puzzle of simply being me. My content is raw, real, and highly transparent. I am unapologetically myself and proud of my life story, where I come from, what I've been through, and where I find myself today. I have evolved into a Chingona who understands that empowered women empower women. We are better in community, stronger within community, and we never leave our own behind. We must always remember to "Plant the seed of empowerment everywhere we go". I feel that my life story and experiences empower women in so many ways. Those who haven't spoken up, those who are trying to figure out how to speak up, and those who have yet to find that voice within themselves to share their stories.

I feel that many women have not had the opportunity to speak out yet, so in a sense I feel like the voice for the voiceless. I encourage others to find it within themselves to begin journaling, in hopes that they can work through that fear, doubt, or any kind of shame that they may be experiencing regarding their life stories. There should never be any shame when we share our life stories. Our life stories are beautiful; they create beautiful masterpieces within us. These life stories give hope to people who have felt alone for years. Our stories are what encourage others to keep going. Our stories become someone else's survival guide, and that is why it is critical that we find our voices and become proud of our journeys. In my story education, positively changed my life. Although, I do have to say that education is not for everyone. I totally respect and understand that. But for me, it worked wonders. For me, it opened doors that I never knew existed and helped me find my voice. It helped me find that strong, brave, brilliant, empowering, powerful Chingona within myself who was always there. I just needed a little help to see it. My education helped me create new, healthy cycles for my children. My education gave me confidence and awakened something inside of me that made me feel like I was, for once in my life, invincible - that I could do so much more and conquer the world. With my story, I have the potential to touch many hearts around the world, and I have indeed done just that.

## Tips:

My advice to you would be:

- Stand in your truth.
- Continue to unapologetically be yourself.
- Create boundaries.
- Stand your ground.
- Never diminish your light to accommodate others.

There's nothing wrong with putting yourself first - your needs, your wants, your desires, and your dreams. Before we became mothers, we were somebody. Don't forget about her. Remember to feed her, nourish her, and give her life again. Another thing that I struggled with was asking for help. That's not a sign of weakness. That is actually a powerful sign of strength. It is very hard to ask for help, but know that there's nothing wrong with doing it. You don't need to face life alone; you have a community behind you. You have people who love you, believe in you, and want what's best for you. So whatever it is that you choose to do, go out there and do it with all of your heart, be intentional, and be authentic. There's something greater out there for all of us. *Todo en su tiempo*. Our time will come - y'all gotta be ready when it presents itself though! Stay working, stay grinding, stay growing, and stay thriving in a world that doesn't wanna see US FLOURISH. **Stay Chingona**. We've got this Chingonas! A chingarle!

# JOIN THE MOVEMENT!
## #HerBusinessHerWealth

## HERBusiness HERWealth

### With Jennifer Lara

Welcome to the world of Her Business Her Wealth, founded by the unstoppable Jennifer Lara in 2022. a trailblazer with a heart dedicated to empowering extraordinary women. Recognizing their immense potential, she became the guiding force they needed to turn their visions into reality. In her eyes, they weren't just dreams; they were world-altering businesses waiting to happen. Jennifer embraced the roles of bridge and catalyst, recognizing that mastering the art of leadership and harnessing the dynamic potential of social media marketing were the keys to unlocking their dreams. Armed with wisdom and expertise, she embarked on a mission: to empower women, helping them transform their unique skills into vibrant careers and businesses. For Jennifer, it's not just about income; it's about creating lives abundant with choices, freedom, and endless opportunities. Join the community and discover the boundless horizons of your potential!

A community of
**AMBITIOUS, TRAILBLAZING FEMALE**
*Entrepreneurs*

Building IMPACTFUL Businesses

WWW.IAMJENLARA.COM

# GROW YOUR BUSINESS WITH US

**Looking to become a sponsor or build a partnership?**

Email us at info@iamjenlara.com